Chicago Catholics
and the Struggles
within Their
Church

Chicago Catholics
and the *Struggles*
within **Their**
Church

Andrew M. Greeley

Transaction Publishers
New Brunswick (U.S.A.) and London (U.K.)

Library of Congress Catalog Number: 2010017601
ISBN: 978-1-4128-1479-9
Printed in the United States of America

Library of Congress Cataloging-in-Publication Data

Greeley, Andrew M., 1928-
    Chicago Catholics and the struggles within their church / Andrew Greeley.
        p. cm.
    Includes bibliographical references and index.
    ISBN 978-1-4128-1479-9
        1. Catholic Church. Archdiocese of Chicago (Ill.)--Public opinion. 2. Catholics--Illinois--Chicago Region--Attitudes. 3. Public opinion--Illinois--Chicago Region. 4. Catholic Church--Public opinion. I. Title.
BX1417.C46G74 2010
282'.77311090511--dc22

                                                    2010017601

This Chicago story is dedicated to the honored memories of Cardinal Albert Meyer who sent me for the first time into the world of the academy.

And Joseph Ficther, S.J. who inaugurated the study of the sociology of a diocese in his suppressed *Southern Parish* project.

Contents

Foreword

What might one expect to find in a probability sample study of the Archdiocese of Chicago? If one consults the conventional wisdom of the local media and listens to the chatter of Chicago's liberal Catholic elite (found for the most part in two wards, the 5th and the 42nd, one would think that the following propositions will be sustained by the data:

1. There will be large numbers of marginal Catholics leaving the Church because of the various scandals in the Church, especially the sexual abuse mess.
2. The intense community sense of the fading ethnic enclaves in the city will be diminishing.
3. Younger Chicago Catholics are drifting into secularist alienation.
4. A sense of Catholic identity is no longer very strong. Chicago Catholics question central Catholic teachings about for instance life after death or the presence of Jesus in the Eucharist or the importance of the sacraments.
5. Catholics are dissatisfied with their leaders from the pope on down to their pastor.
6. Most of those who have left the Church are unlikely to return to it.
7. Chicago Catholics give their local clergy low grades on professionalism.
8. Tension over the Church's sexual ethic has alienated the laity.
9. Intermarriage rates are high among Chicago Catholics.
10. Most Chicago Catholics are not committed to raising their children as Catholics.
11. Catholic schools are no longer important in Chicago.

These eleven propositions will seem unexceptionable to many Chicago Catholics who will wonder why anyone would waste good money trying to find data to support them. Why bother? Everyone knows they're true? Then why bother with the project? What the Archdiocese needs from a sociologist is an indictment that will wake up the leaders of the Archdiocese. You don't need to interview a probability sample of half a thousand respondents, do you?

The only problem with that eleven-pronged indictment is that none of the propositions happen to be true.

1. About 25 percent of people in our sample were once Catholic and have left the Church, however, the reasons they left are not the mass media ones.
2. Almost half the Catholics in the sample report that their five closest friends are Catholic.
3. Despite the minimal money and resources that the Church invests in young people, the youngest cohort is in many respects more devout and dedicated than any of its predecessors.
4. Chicago Catholics have strong identity; four out of five say their religion is "very important" or "extremely important" to them. Their identity is built around concern for the poor, Jesus in the Eucharist, belief in the Resurrection, devotion to Mary the Mother of Jesus, and the presence of God in the sacraments
5. Four-fifths of Chicago Catholics approve of the pope, the Cardinal, and their pastor.
6. Forty percent of the lost sheep are open to the possibility of return to the sheepfold.
7. Chicago Catholics strongly support the professional performance of their clergy.
8. With astonishing ease, Chicago Catholics have separated what God demands of them and what the Church expects of them.
9. Three-fifths of Chicago Catholics are married to other Catholics; four-fifths are raising their children Catholic.
10. Ninety-five percent of Chicago Catholics are raising (or have raised) their Children as Catholic. Nearly all Catholic couples are raising their children in the faith, and 79 percent of the children in mixed marriages are being raised Catholic.
11. Four-fifths of adult Catholics have attended Catholic schools some of the time. Attendance at such school has considerable impact on Catholic laity.

It does not follow from the above findings that all is well in the Archdiocese. Very few young people plan to be a priest or a nun. Cafeteria Catholicism divides the Catholic population into two groups. Catholic schools are closing. Many dispense themselves from Sunday Mass because they get nothing out of it, because it is dull, tedious, and BORING! The reformed rites of the Sunday liturgy are usually not more vital than the old Latin Mass. For all the ideologies with which the liturgists try to indoctrinate the congregation, the power and the possibility of the new liturgy has not been given a chance to become a prayer interlude to which people flock because it is inspiring and graceful. Work with and for teens and young adults languishes while many "young" priests pay little attention to the future generations. There is simply, they say, not enough time—an excuse not without some validity. Only the most minimal efforts are expended which might attract the young laity. Pastors continue to fight off the laity who, they suspect, are trying to take away the parish from them.

The vitality to be reported in this book suggests that there are great strengths and powerful resources in the Archdiocese. Many Chicago Catholics, lay and clerical, will resent what they see as good news that's too good to be true. Good news, alas, demands more work at a time when there is already too much work.

Both the left, which thinks Chicago Catholics should be more resentful of their leadership, and the right, which thinks that Catholics are more orthodox—or should be—on sexual issues, will try to cast doubts on the study. Both will say that no one in their family or none of their friends were interviewed—as if such events would make the sample valid. Others will complain that the findings aren't clear-cut enough. The study, they will say, is mired in grayness—as if the real world in which people live and love and work out their salvation is not complex.

Later in the book we will discuss reasons to believe that the study is reasonably accurate. The best answer to those who question the validity of this report is that if they don't trust the integrity or the professionalism of the researchers ,they should use their own money to do their own study.

Why study Chicago? Can one estimate a national portrait of Catholics in the United States from data about Chicago? Comparisons between Chicago and the rest of the Catholic population may show how unique the city is, for example, in its judgments about its clergy. It may also make possible comparisons with studies that someday might be made between Chicago Catholics and other Catholic subpopulations. The findings in this study suggest that history and geography may provide not only a background for the development of the Catholic Church in a specific area but might also be factors that shape, to a considerable extent, that development. The late Jesuit sociologist, Joseph Fichter once observed that creative Catholicism in the United States took place in a triangle drawn between St. John's Abbey in Minnesota, the University of Notre Dame, and Chicago (perhaps an ungainly triangle). A madcap cardinal later destroyed all creativity he could find in Chicago but did not, it would seem from this research project, destroy the unique attitudes of the Chicago laity towards their clergy.

Will comparative studies of other dioceses provide not only important insights into the development of immigrant religion but also open up further investigations into the sociology of religion and the sociology of religious leadership? The answer to that question is a blunt "no."

The current bench of bishops is terrified of research which, because the men sitting on the bench (most of whom should have been left back in the locker room) have learned to expect nothing but bad news from research. So they pretend it doesn't exist or dismiss it with a cliché. It does not matter that much of the research reports good news. My credibility as a sociologist was wiped out when I began to report that most of the Catholic laity (everywhere in the world) was not honoring the birth control teaching. I was told that a priest sociologist should not report what people were doing but what they *should* be doing. Despite all the good news about Chicago Catholics in this book, I must nevertheless report that the majority of Catholic laity in Chicago (as elsewhere) no longer accepts the Catholic sexual ethic. However, they remain devoutly Catholic. They can't do that, the leadership replies. Sometimes they add the hope that the pope will get rid of those non-conformist laity so that the Catholic Church will become "smaller, leaner, and purer and more Catholic."

The proper answer to such exclusivist daydreams is, "What if they won't leave?" Forty years after the birth control encyclical, and they still have not left, not in this country (Greeley 2000; 2004a), certainly not in Chicago, and they show no signs of leaving. Nor are they likely to accept efforts to throw them out.

Will this report provide any help to those priests and laity who are working in the Archdiocese of Chicago? Would not that be sufficient reason for writing it? For some people, perhaps (not many clergy). But most Chicago priests gave up on me long ago. Why then bother?

The late Cardinal Albert Meyer sent me to graduate school to learn sociology so I could study the Archdiocese. He was succeeded by Cardinal John Cody who did not need a sociologist or anyone else to help him. Thereupon I disappeared, even from the directory of Chicago priests for some years. This is a project I've always wanted to do and for which I was trained a half century ago. It occurred to me as I approached my eightieth birthday that time was running out and that no one has approached me from the Archdiocese demanding that I exercise my alleged skills as a sociologist and offering to defer the costs. So if I was to study the sociology of the Archdiocese I'd better do it myself while there was still time.[1]

Priests will ask me, as they always have, why did you write that report, thus attempting to shift the focus from the findings to my motives. My answer: "Because I wanted to." As is clear by now, I will make no effort to write this book with a pose of detachment. There are some kinds of monographs in which the author should not let his emotions show. I have established a lengthly reputation for not being one such author, at least on this topic. I'm too old to change.

Catholicism, before it becomes creed and law, is a combination of story, community, and hierarchy. These three dimensions will weave their way through my report. I will argue that the official Church in Chicago has not recognized the community structures that permeate the neighborhoods (and, hence, has not sufficiently appreciated its parishes) that it does not grasp the religious stories that shape the people's identity and does not understand the intense, if selective, loyalty of the archdiocese to its leadership.

After reporting the findings from the survey, I append transcriptions of some of the in-depth interviews of former Catholics, as it were, to flesh out the statistical bones.

I wish to acknowledge the wise and indispensable help of Professor Colm O'Muircheartaigh (late of the Kingdom of Kerry) for his liaison with the Survey Laboratory of the University of Chicago, for designing the sample, and for refreshing the work with his irresistible West of Ireland wit.

Michael Hout, my mentor in all matters sociological, has always been ready for a phone call.

I have depended over the years on my Arizona colleague Professor Margaret Kenski for loyal friendship, insightful advice, and wise direction during the project's early phases.

I am grateful to the Survey Lab and its directors, Kelly Daley, Martha VanHaitsma, and Kevin Ulrich, and for the gifted young men and women who carried out the project with elegance and grace, to my assistant Roberta Wilk and my research assistant Emily Dolan for sustaining the momentum of the project while I flitted around my world.

Note

1. The Chicago Catholics study was designed and analyzed by Andrew Greeley. He completed his analysis of the study in October 2008 shortly before being injured in an accident in November 2008. Minor editorial refinements were made to his manuscript with the assistance of Tom W. Smith, NORC/University of Chicago; Colm O'Muircheartaigh, University of Chicago; Michael Hout, University of California, Berkeley; Sean Durkin, Chicago Partners; and Roberta Wilk, Greeley's administrative assistant. It should be reiterated that *Chicago Catholics and the Struggles within Their Church* is, in the final analysis, the work of Andrew Greeley.

Introduction: The Archdiocese by the Lake

The Catholic Archdiocese of Chicago is composed of two counties, Lake and Cook, pushed up against Lake Michigan by the encroaching suburban dioceses of Joliet[1] and Rockford, which greedily absorb as many of Chicago's Catholics as can be lured out of the City and out of Cook County. At the same time the Catholic population has been pushed up against the boundary of DuPage County by racial change in the city, so that much of the west and south side Catholic population of the city has moved into the southern and western suburbs. Approximately half of the 2.5 million Catholics within the boundaries of Cook and Lake Counties are suburbanites. Moreover, in this research, half of the Catholics have attended college and half of that half have attended graduate school. One cannot simply say that the Archdiocese of Chicago has become suburban and college educated, but one must say that such folks are a major component population of the Archdiocese. Thus, the conventional image of Chicago as a congeries of ethnic immigrant neighborhoods has faded somewhat, though there are still many new immigrants attending special immigrant parishes or special masses for immigrants in existing parishes. As I will note later, many if not most of the lost sheep are immigrants or the children of immigrants.

As one might suspect the ties of ethnic neighborhood diminish somewhat as educational attainment increases. Half of those who did not go beyond high school said that all of their five closest friends were Catholic, as opposed to 37 percent of those who attended college, and 28 percent of those who attended graduate school. However, 53 percent of those who attended college said that at least four of their five closest friends were Catholic, as did 44 percent of those who had attended graduate school (and 63 percent of the graduate school Catholics said that three of their closest friends were Catholic). Approximately a quarter of all Catholics, regardless of education, say that at least these three of these closest friends live or at least once lived in the same neighborhood. The neighborhoods, at least in memory if not in actual reality, are still strong structural constraints in the Archdiocese. There are no data available on neighborhood influences among those who are not Catholics[2]or Catholics who live in other large metropolitan areas. However, it is not likely that one would find such tight-knit ecclesiastical communities in most American locales. Catholicism is of course a communal religion. Despite happy talk among some Catholic liberals about the end of the "old neighborhood," it seems alive and well in Chicago, though in somewhat modified forms. Moreover, this rampant communalism is not affected by age. There is no correlation between age and close friends that are Catholic. Indeed, in every one of our four cohorts (Before 1935, 1936-1960, 1961-1975, 1976-1989) approximately two-fifths of Chicago Catholics say that their five best friends are Catholic.[3] This is communalism with a vengeance. Are Catholics too clannish, as we on the West Side used to say to our South Side rivals, or merely loyal as they used to reply to us? Whatever the label used, this dimension of Chicago Catholic life is critically important to understanding what Catholicism in Chicago is like.

Chicago Catholics are also slightly younger than the national average for Catholics. The average age of Chicago Catholics is forty-four, a year less than for the general population, and two years younger than the average for all Americans. Seventeen percent of Chicago Catholics identify as Irish, 13 percent as Hispanic, 11 percent as Polish, 8 percent as Italian 4 percent as German, 4 percent as African American, 2 percent as "Other Eastern European," and 39 percent as "mixed."

The "Hispanic" proportion is obviously too low. The United States Census identifies almost a million Hispanics in the City of Chicago. However, given the understandable distrust in the Hispanic community for people who ask questions about ethnic origins, estimates about them from survey data must be made very cautiously.

The typical Chicago Catholic has had 5.8 years of Catholic school. Eighteen percent graduated from Catholic high schools. Two-thirds pray every day (thirteen percentage points higher than national average). Eighty-nine percent claim that they contributed to their parish last year, and 31 percent that they contributed to the Cardinal's annual appeal. Fifty-four percent are married, 80 percent by a priest,[4] 80 percent are raising their children Catholic, and half of the children are in Catholic schools. Seventy-eight percent say that Catholicism is either "extremely important" or "very important" in their lives.

A very complicated place, this Archdiocese of Chicago—ethnic, college educated, young, suburban, intensely communal, and presumably loyal. As evidence of their loyalty, they tend to be married in the presence of a priest, and two-thirds of them have married other Catholics. They raise their children as Catholics and claim to contribute to the Church. They have on the average 2.52 children, way above the national averages and 37 percent have 3 or more children.

One might sympathize with the leadership in the Archdiocese—how do you cope with such a crowd of loyal, dedicated, well-educated people, especially when they tend to think for themselves on some critical ethical issues. Yet, one must add to that symphony that they tend to be deeply embedded in the Catholic community and that communal loyalty ought to be praised, celebrated, and respected.

Chicago Catholics tend to be enthusiastic about their leaders, an enthusiasm that will seem too many to go beyond right reason. The respondents were asked the standard blunt political question—"Do you approve or disapprove of the job being done by the pastor of your parish...by the bishop Cardinal Francis George...by the Pope Benedict XVI?"

Eighty-five percent approved of the pope, 86 percent of the Cardinal and 90 percent of the pastor. Moreover the only statistically significant correlations with age, education, and gender were a .20 between education and approval of the pope with "only" two-thirds of the graduate school at attendees approving of Benedict's job performance. The survey paralleled a "media scandal" over a somewhat tardy resolution of a sexual abuse problem in a Chicago parish. A leader in SNAP (Survivor's Network of Abuse by Priests) used this event to call for the Cardinal's resignation, a call which a religion writer mentioned on every possible occasion as though it were part of a wave of discontent among Chicago Catholics. SNAP and Voice of the Faithful (another protest group on sexual abuse) launched a campaign to defeat the Cardinal's election as President of the American hierarchy.[5] Yet this "scandal" seemed to have no effect on the Cardinal's popularity with the people.

I trust that my reputation for disagreeing with and criticizing Cardinals, bishops, and my fellow priests will establish that I have no vested interest in promoting high approval ratings for the hierarchy. I confess that I was surprised by this enthusiasm among Chicago Catholics for their leadership. However two other data collection efforts substantiate the findings reported here, a pre-test in depth of a hundred respondents carried out by an Arizona data collection agency (of Catholics in Cook and Lake County) last year and a "secret" study done by the Archdiocese at about the same time as this project which apparently matches my findings.[6]

One can therefore exclude the possibility that there was a bias in the data collection by the University of Chicago Survey lab. There remains, however, the possibility that the Chicago Catholic laity is so strong in their loyalty to the Church that they will either exaggerate the skills of their leaders when they sense criticism or at least give them the benefit of the doubt.

This question will recur frequently in the present book. It is worth noting, however, as the data in chapter 2 show some Catholics have been so upset with their leaders as to leave the Church, others have at least thought about leaving, and most do not accept certain Catholic teachings or the infallibility of the pope.

Chicago Catholics are loyal, extremely loyal, exceptionally loyal, but neither blind nor unthinking.

Notes

1. Joliet is one of the largest dioceses in the country. Its center of population and wealth DuPage County is closer to the Chicago Loop than it is to Joliet and DuPage lives off the wealth of the Metropolitan Area. Its people look to Chicago as their central city. The commuter trains from DuPage all run to the Loop and not to Joliet. This bizarre situation can be traced to decisions that were made in 1949 when the Joliet Diocese was carved out of Chicago and Rockford. DuPage was given to Chicago and Lake to Rockford to make up for the counties it lost to Joliet. But Cardinal Samuel Stritch did not want his seminary (St. Mary of the Lake at Mundelein Illinois) to be technically within another diocese. He therefore, without any consultation, it is said, traded DuPage for Lake, a very unfortunate decision even then. Chicago would be perhaps one of the largest and most affluent dioceses in the world. However, it would have today the difficult task of finding enough priests to staff all the parishes in DuPage.
2. "Publics" as we used to call them and still do and as they often call themselves at least when talking to us. Much better than the abomination from our youth of "non-Catholic."
3. The national average (from NORC's General Social Survey) is 2 percent of Catholics in the United States report that all five of their closest friends are Catholic. Another 2 percent say that four of their five closest friends are Catholic and 17 percent report that three of their five closest friends are Catholic.
4. In the presence of a priest, since in Catholic theory the spouses administer the sacrament to one another.
5. He was elected on the first ballot with 85 percent of the vote.
6. I will discuss this survey subsequently.

1

Destabilization of Structures in the Local Church

In *The Catholic Revolution* (Greeley, 2004a) I proposed a theory, based on the "event sociology" propounded by William Sewell (1996) that Vatican Council II was a revolutionary event that destabilized the structures of the Catholic Church—habits of routine behavior and supporting motivations, e.g. Sunday Church attendance supported by the fear of mortal sin and hellfire for failure to attend. In this book, I propose to investigate the revolutionary event as it has affected one archdiocese in the United States.

The Vatican curialists rejected such an explanation.[1] The council was not a rupture with the past but a continuation. The documents of the council could be authoritatively interpreted only by the "magisterium," theoretically the pope and the bishops but practically the pope and the curia. A proper understanding of the Church's teachings could be found not in the documents of the council but in the *Catechism of the Catholic Church*. Nothing had changed.

"Rupture" was a deceptive word. No one claimed that the Catholic tradition had been ruptured. However, it had been dramatically changed. John Courtney Murray S.J., who drafted the council's document on religious liberty, *Dignitatis Humanae* had been forbidden to write or speak on the subject only a few years before the council convened. He had been "disinvited" to the first session and attended the second only because of the patronage of Cardinal Francis Spellman. Yet, as one of its most important theologians, he had concelebrated the concluding Eucharist with Pope Paul VI. Seldom had the Church changed a traditional teaching so quickly and so dramatically.[2] The opponents of the council, like the Society of Pius X which broke with the Church, refuses to be drawn back in by the possibility of the Mass in Latin again. *Dignitatis Humanae* must be repealed and repudiated.

If one grants the theory of the curialists that nothing has changed, one must still contend that tremendous destabilization has occurred around the Catholic world. If one introduces the yeast of change into an institution, the resultant changes, perhaps not explicitly intended by the Council fathers, will be dramatic and perhaps traumatic. Secure in their dicasteries and supported by their own handpicked bishops around the world, the curialists can hardly deny the changes, as much as they rail against them. Church attendance has declined even in traditionally Catholic countries. Vocations to the priesthood and religious life have diminished. The laity in every country on which data are available (including Second- and Third-World countries, including Poland) generally ignore the Church's sexual ethic and pay little attention to Roman documents.[3]

I argued in *The Catholic Revolution* that the destabilization has become worse, precisely because Church leadership apparently cannot admit to itself that such changes are occurring. One must blame the erosions of the past forty years not on the council or the council fathers, but on the curialists for their denial of the ferment and their failure to support sensitive and nuanced implementations of the council. One can understand their desire to reassure the timid laity and themselves, but the price of such reassurance is burying their heads in the sands of denial. Repetition of jeremiads against "secularism" and "relativism" have little impact.

In this book I intend to examine the destabilization of religious structures in the Archdiocese of Chicago to determine whether and to what extent the Sewell model must be applied to a vigorous Catholic diocese in the United States and how the Catholic laity of Chicago has reacted to the stresses and strains of the changes.[4]

In 1970 there were 1141 diocesan priests, 8331 religious women, and 1607 seminarians[5] in the Archdiocese. In 2006 there were 839 priests, 2397 religious women, and 348 seminarians. If ever there was evidence of destabilization of structures, it is to be found in those numbers. Should the Council Fathers be blamed? Should the secularist, relativist laity be blamed? Or should the curialists who stonewalled the full implementation of the Council? If you're in Rome, of course, you blame the Catholic laity.

Churches that were packed on Sundays are now half-empty. Rectories, which once housed four priests, now have only one. More than half the priests are from outside of the Archdiocese, most of them from outside the country (Asia, Africa, and Poland). Young priests, the traditional ministers to the young, have virtually disappeared. The more mature vocations are often, as Hoge (2001) has reported, more likely to think of themselves as qualitatively different from the laity and that the laity must be taught to obey them. Ordination is less a challenge to ministry than the conferring of an identity. The Southwest Side and its adjoining suburbs, once a seedbed of priestly vocations, have not produced a new priest for many years.

To make matters worse the American Church, including Chicago, has been plagued by the sexual abuse crisis, a phenomenon which as we will see in this book has profoundly angered many Catholics." In Chicago—after the stonewalling ended "credible accusations" were brought against priests of whom most have subsequently been removed from the priesthood. The practice of reassigning accused priests to new parishes ended in the late nineteen nineties. However, the charges against priests continues as does the payment of money to victims. In fact, the 4 percent of priests who have been charged is no higher than in other denominations or among teachers or athletic coaches. The anger of the laity is against the bishops who tried to cover up and reassign suspect priests.

Simultaneously, some bishops have ruled that it is seriously sinful to vote for a political candidate who support policies to which the church is opposed—abortion, gay marriage, artificial insemination. Others have ruled that Catholic politicians who do not vote against such policies should not receive the Eucharist. Such bishops are accused of hypocrisy for tolerating abusive priests and condemning politicians who are making crucial and painful political decisions. In Chicago, this has meant only that priests are told not to give communion to gay couples who present themselves in the rainbow sashes (and many priests ignore such instructions). Some priests also refuse the sacraments to politicians but most others do not do so.

Moreover, the laity are troubled by the constant fussing with the Sunday liturgy, which they think to be an obsession with the trivial, while Rome burns.

Yet if one goes back a half century, one remembers a very different Church. The parish and the precinct were the centers of life in the ethnic neighborhoods. The churches were filled on Sundays, the school halls on weekday nights with various meetings or athletic events. There were separate organizations for men and women (Holy Name Society to fight blasphemy and Altar and Rosary Society to keep the church neat and clean) and perhaps an organization for young men and women to come in contact with one another for possible marriage. In some parishes there would be a high club or teen club, though such ventures were not durable because teens made noise and mess, to both of which janitors and sisters superior strongly objected. There was always a building fund for new or renewed construction.

A Catholic identity included fish on Friday, mass on Sunday, and no birth control. Typically on Saturday afternoon and evenings, confessions continued for two hours in the afternoon and an hour and a half in the evenings and the whole school was processed through the confessionals on the Thursday before first Friday, a practice which violated the young people's rights and verged on blasphemy.

Perhaps a little more than half of the parish went to church every week, and half of that received Communion. At Christmas and Easter, most of the parish turned out for Mass and received Communion. The non-communicants labeled themselves as people who were having "problems with birth control." Divorced and remarried Catholics were denied the sacraments and were described as "living in sin," an embarrassment to themselves and especially to their children.

Every couple of years, "missionaries" were brought into the parish to rekindle the faith and morality of their people, though to those of us who had to hear confessions, all they did was stir up scruples about past "bad" confessions. We used to reflect that it took several months after the missionaries had departed to settle the parish down and to persuade the people that God was not trying to trick his people into hell.

Grammar school graduation was the high point of the school year, when, not without some relief, the parish sent the eighth graders off to high school, having fulfilled its major educational obligation.

Stations of the cross were said during lent, benediction of the blessed sacrament (and the Sorrowful Mother Novena) took place every Friday evening. Dispensations from Lenten fast and abstinence were given, often times ungraciously, to those who were going away for a week of sun. Ashes were distributed on Ash Wednesday and throats were blessed on the Feast of St. Blaise. If you were Irish, your pastor was likely to violate all rules and wear green vestments at Mass—a custom that has not disappeared altogether. Masses were also said on the "Holy Days of Obligation" (originally Holy Days of Celebration) and many people showed up at Church or down in the Loop, though the obligation was not take so seriously as the Sunday obligation. Some devout Catholics of my generation are furious at the bishops and priests for "fooling around" with the obligations—as well they might be. The biggest offense, however, was the elimination of the Friday abstinence obligation—a harmless symbol that was destroyed simply because it was there. Everything seemed to unravel after that.

Birth control declined as a problem for people in 1965. Most younger Catholics today can't believe that it was an issue that created so much anguish for their parents and grandparents. Yet, when the church eliminated fish on Friday and priests generally eliminated birth control (and masturbation too) everything did unravel. Mortal sin and hellfire no longer frightened younger Catholics. People went to confession less often because it seemed there were fewer things to confess.

Those of us who achieved what passed for maturity before the council and then lived through its heady years would not have believed that the Chicago parish I have described would ever change. Some of us were furious at its passing, others delighted, still others confused. We have gradually been replaced by the demographic processes according to which the young arrive and the older depart. I confess I miss the crowded churches and the young priests and the chaste young people, but I don't—and won't ever—miss the fear and the absence of the God who is love. If it all had to go down the drain to recover the insight that Deus Caritas Est, then it had to go. The point is that loss of the overarching power of Mortal Sin as the universal motive for being a Catholic and keeping the Catholic rules is not a bad thing. Though many of the older laity are not yet prepared to let it go.

The overwhelming majority of American Catholics liked the changes that the council created. Seven out of eight approved of the English mass. Most, even the elderly, approved of the "change" in birth control—even though it was a change of which the Vatican did not pronounce, but which the laity embraced nonetheless. In the early seventies, 29 percent of American Catholics thought that premarital sex was never wrong, in the early 21st century that has risen to 43 percent, validation perhaps of the "hook-up" sexual culture. In the same era, the proportion thinking that homosexual sex is always wrong has declined from 69 percent to just under 50 percent.[6]

It is not fair to say the laity in Chicago or anywhere else are polarized. In the rapid change of the last several decades, there has been a polarization of ideologies on the Vatican Council. There is a segment of the Catholic population that would like to return to the status quo ante, either because they miss it or because they miss it without having experienced it and yearn for artificial nostalgia. The Latin Mass is so elegant and graceful. Marian devotions are so lovely.[7] However, it is unlikely that the restorationists constitute more than the 10 percent of the population still convinced that birth control is wrong. Much of the reaction to the "New Church" is not ideological. Most Catholic laity are not inclined to sign on either with the Voice of the Faithful or the Faithful Voice, either with the Call to Action or Opus Dei, either with pro-life or pro-choice groups or to subscribe either to the *National Catholic Reporter* or the *Wanderer*, either to *First Things* or *The Commonweal*. This pragmatic and extremely large Catholic middle may be the lukewarm that Jesus would vomit out of his mouth or they may be the wise ones who have better things to do with their time than become involved in internal Catholic "politics" as they see it, like earn a living and raise their children, and keep the marital boat from rocking too much.

Yet the dissidents on the right are always around—in Chicago there are two Opus Dei high schools (and one Jesuit High school that uses an Opus text book for a sophomore religion text book) and one High School run by the Legionnaires of Christ (whose founder was in effect suspended from public ministry after serious pedophile charges). There is Mother Angelica's Eternal Word TV channel and her flock of strange looking clergy. There is the occasional retreat or day of recollection master who wants to talk about birth control or masturbation or the "missionary" who denounces youthful yearning for sex. There are the Catholics United for the Faith who harass college and university faculties and the Newman Society, which goes after individual scholars.

These kinds of folks—who certainly have the right to their convictions and beliefs and the right to push them—are part of the Chicago Catholic environment. Once upon a time, there was little evidence of such polarization or the zeal of, let us say, folk such as the Voice of the Faithful (VOTF) which wants to blackball bishops from holding office in the national hierarchy. Part of the struggle of Chicago Catholics is to fend off such, as they see it, zealots.

Nationally the more important struggles for the mass middle of the Catholic laity are against bishops who harass them with political instructions, interminable pastoral letters (written to win approval from their masters in Rome) and seem unwilling to apologize or resign because of the mess they have made in their dioceses—either financial or administrative or in matters of sex abuse. The laity also stand against priests who have turned the reception of the sacraments—especially marriage and baptism—into obstacle courses, extra-canonical hoops through which the laity are made to jump, often several times, before they can receive the sacraments; against priests who do not know how to smile; against priests who are rude and insulting; against priests who are unable to put together a single sentence of decent prose for a sermon; and finally against priests who still believe that possessing a roman collar makes them a lord of creation.

Having said that, one must also add that large majorities of Chicago Catholics give high marks to their parish priest, to the Cardinal, and to the pope. Most are not about to leave the Church, no matter how sick they might be of the incompetence of its leaders.

The middle mass of Chicago Catholics about whom I will report in this book like being Catholic and even like, more or less, their clergy. The de-stabilization continues and will probably continue for a long time. There are very serious problems and problems with which Chicago Catholics must wrestle. Chastity (not the same thing as celibacy) and regular church attendance are serious problems. Respect for women is of utmost importance and not just to ideological feminists and the Church in Chicago has not made much progress in demonstrating to women that it knows that its women problem is very serious. In retrospect, the good old days seem simple and, to tell the truth, dull.[8]

Notes

1. My own claim that the council was "eventful" has been ignored. I am too much a minor league player to be taken seriously.
2   One commentator calls this kind of doctrinal change an exercise in "selective amnesia." It must be very powerful amnesia to forget the thunder against religious freedom in the Syllabus of Errors.
3. At the time of the drafting of this book, a retired Australian bishop has issued a book which criticizes the sexual ethic and the exercise of power in the Church, a group of Dutch Dominicans have urged the Netherlanders to organize their own parishes, select their own priests, and demand that bishops ordain them, only 18,000 Austrian Catholics came out to welcome the pope's visit to Vienna, and the German hierarchy has rejected a "definitive" document from the Congregation for the Defense of the Faith on other religions.
4. The present book is based on data from five hundred Catholic respondents in Cook and Lake Counties contacted by the Social Science Survey Lab at the University of Chicago in the summer and autumn of 2007. (See Appendix A for a sample design by Professor Colm O'Muircheartaigh.) In the spring of the same year I had commissioned a pretest of a hundred respondents to be conducted by a firm in Arizona to determine whether the project was feasible. As luck (i.e. probability statistics) would have it, the pretest numbers came very close to those of the final study. Rather than combine the two surveys, I have kept them separate so that I can appeal to the pretest to show that the findings of the survey lab were not the result of an error, especially when a given finding seemed unlikely. Thus in the present study, conducted during the "surge" in the Iraq war, 44 percent of Catholics in the Archdiocese of Chicago thought that a "good Catholic" had to take seriously the

pope's teachings on war and peace. For a population that paid little attention to his teachings on the death penalty, this seemed quite high. In the pretest population the response was 47 percent. In general the same confirmation occurs in all suspect responses. Chicago Catholics might be exaggerating their piety, but they were answering the survey lab interviewers the same way they had answered the pretest interviewers.

5.   Including students at high school seminaries, both of which have been closed.
6.   Source: NORC General Social Survey, n=30, 397.
7.   The Liturgists have made many serious mistakes as they try to reshape the American laity in their own image and likeness, but non more serious than trying to squeeze the Mother of Jesus out of Catholic devotion life as we shall see subsequently.
8.   Why did I commission this study and why have I written this book to summarize its findings? That is a question my fellow priests will ask, hoping to shift the issue from the findings of the researcher to his motives. To answer the question once and for all, I wanted to find out more about Chicago Catholics, which is my right as a sociologist and a priest of the Archdiocese. I was sent to graduate school by Cardinal Meyer to learn how to do sociology and then study the Archdiocese. Then because of his early death and various changes in the Church, the Archdiocese had no use for its own sociologist and did its best to forget about his existence. I also became, in the process, an expert on the sociology of Catholic schools, defending the schools against those in the Catholic education elite who had lost confidence in them. They were not, it was said, what the Church needed "after the council." Neither the Archdiocese nor the school office to this day has asked my sociological opinion on anything. So my study of the Archdiocese of Chicago, planned in 1962 when I graduated with my very own PH.D, was never done. It was therefore possible for anyone and everyone to generalize about the Church in Chicago without any data to support such generalizations. The only research was an annual "October Count" of the average number of people in Catholic churches during the Sundays of October. Such a dubious method—which seemed to assume that the same number people were in church every Sunday, though anyone with an ounce of sense knew that such an assumption was not a valid one. But, it was argued, a useful if crude indicator of the ups and downs of church attendances in various parishes. At best the result of the October Count (going on once again as I write this footnote) is a fact, not an explanation that provides self-anointed experts free rein to project their own biases, opinions, and paranoia into the data. I shake my head in disbelief that no one has ever bothered to ask why Church attendance has declined, either in Chicago or anywhere else. I do not flatter myself that the explanations I will offer in this book will gain any credibility and acceptance. I would also hope that other dioceses might find a way to replicate this study so that sometime in the future a comparative study of Catholic dioceses might become possible. It is also possible, but not likely, that Chicago clergy might not say, well, we don't have that problem here. Finally, and I suppose most important, I had wanted to do this study for all my life as a sociologist. Entering my ninth decade, I figure it was time to do it.

I have since discovered that the chancery is doing its own study. Naturally, no one asked me what I thought. I am told that they are not going to make public their findings. With the help of God and the Chicago River not rising, this project will be made public.

2

The Lost Sheep

A little less than one-quarter of those who fell into the Survey Lab sample were former Catholics (400 thousand lost lambs). We do not know when they left the Church, whether they were born Catholics, or converts who changed their minds or how long they may have been Catholics. We do know why they left and that they have little intention of returning. Some of them are very angry, perhaps with good reason. They bear witness to the mistakes the Church has made with some of its people and are perhaps a unique sample of those who have left us with, to put it mildly, a clear conscience. The alert young staff of the survey lab not only coded their responses but also jotted down the substance of their explanation.

We observe in Table 2.1 that, with the exception of the most popular rationale for leaving (Another Church is more appealing) the reasons

Table 2.1
Reasons for Leaving the Church
(% a lot or some)

Another Church more appealing	61%
Insensitive priests	60%
Sex abuse scandal	56%
Too much politics	61%
Church obsessed with money	56%
Role of women in Church	51%
Untrustworthy bishops	50%
Birth control teaching	44%
Abortion teaching	42%
Don't believe any more	41%
Vatican Council	39%
Spouse belongs to another Church	26%
Too much change	21%

given to an open ended question are a characteristic of the modern indictment of the Church—insensitive priests, the sex abuse crisis, untrustworthy bishops, birth control and abortion, and the role of women in the Church. In a factor analysis (an effort to sort out patterns among the responses) two powerful sets of predictors emerged—an abortion/birth-control/role-of-women factor and a factor loading on priests, bishops, sex-abuse, and obsessed with money. The former factor correlates with gender and the second with gender, age, and college attendance. Those who are more likely to have left Catholicism are more likely to be younger (50 percent versus 41 percent), college educated (56 percent versus 43 percent), and women than the typical respondents who are not Catholic in the sample. Fourteen percent of the lost sheep indicate that they might seriously consider returning. Ten percent more do not want to exclude the possibility of return and twenty percent think it is unlike that they will ever return. Fifty-six percent say they absolutely will not return. With the limited number of cases available none of these correlations are statistically significant. However, they point in the direction of a conclusion that suggests the ones most likely to have left the Church lived in suburban Cook and Lake County are younger, better educated, and women. They have been influenced negatively by their experience of Catholicism and/or stereotypes of Catholicism in the media.

Since only a handful (14 percent) show any interest in an immediate return to Catholicism and indeed, as their comments which follow indicate a high degree of hostility, any organized attempt to reclaim them is not likely to be successful until they find the prospect of return more appealing than it is now. Minimally, more priests that are sensitive and trustworthy bishops should be involved. Perhaps even a Church that is more attractive.

Appendix C contains transcripts of interviews with those who have left the church. One might wish to argue that they are troubled men and women taking out their familial conflicts on the church and speaking in stereotypes. One might insist that they stubbornly turned their backs on grace. Nonetheless, such responses should perhaps be considered as self-serving and inappropriate for religious leaders claiming to be evangelizers.

I confess that I am surprised and shocked by the percentage of Catholics who have left the Church. It is double that reported only a few years ago. The recent change, according to Michael Hout, is part of a general drift away from religious affiliation in the most recent cohorts because of repugnance for right wing religious politics. In Hout's work the drift is stronger among Protestant young people. For neither Protestants nor Catholics does it mean a decline in religious faith, only in affiliation. It is not possible to determine whether our resigned are part of this same phenomenon. It also should be noted that there is no reason to believe that that untrustworthy bishop would be a Chicago bishop, since, as we shall see, the Cardinal's approval rating is very high as is the rating of the local pastor (though not necessarily the pastor of the former Catholics interviewed in this survey). These disillusioned, young, educated Catholics are out there. Those who do the Church's work should be alert to the possibility of encountering them. Besides 14 percent of those who were once Catholic is a lot of people.

estions to 1500, 1000, or 500 it is not unlikely that Catholics
eras would react with similar profiles.

he thing must be said of the Archdiocese of Chicago—any
of Catholics who treasure this kind of religious imagination,
ther problems that might exist, is still profoundly (though not
Catholic.

a sort out into three factors—A Social Justice Factor, which
oncern for the poor as well as emphasis on social justice; a
aagination factor, which includes all the other variables down
yer and angels and saints; and a Catholic Organization factor,
ades the rest of the variables—abortion, confession weekly
lible pope, and celibate priesthood. Michael Hout has sug-
the first factor could be named "Peter" because it suggests
t to mission, the Second "Mary" (of Bethany) because it sug-
mitment to spiritual values, and the third "Martha" because
commitment to an orderly household. Both the Martha and
s correlate with youthfulness, gender, and college education.
vomen, and those who have attended college, are more likely
dentities that emphasize spiritual values *and* organizational
aps because their generations are more likely to take sides in
ons. However, unless a doubling of the case base produces
relations, one cannot say that either factor is disproportion-
ed by any of the demographic groups.

if one considers individual variables, there are some inter-
ations; the college educated are less likely to endorse God
nents, Jesus in the Eucharist, the resurrection of Jesus, but
ortance of the pope, the importance of rejecting abortion,
ortance of angels and saints. Women, however, are more
orse as part of their identity Mary the Mother of Jesus, the
thood, daily prayer, and the importance of angels, saints,
stice.

3

Catholic Identities

There is considerable discussion in higher-level Catholic circles
currently about Catholic identity. It was easy in the old days. Catholics
went to Church every Sunday, ate fish every Friday, did not practice
birth control, and tried to marry other Catholics. They also contributed
to the support of their pastor, no matter how much they disliked him.
That doesn't work anymore.

How does one recognize a Catholic school or university, a Catholic
hospital, a Catholic today? Many different people and groups of people
are willing to define Catholic identity on a priori norms. A Catholic
university does not permit gay and lesbian and transsexual clubs. Nor
does it permit performances of *The Vagina Monologues*. A Catholic
hospital does not permit abortions or the distribution of birth control
pills. A Catholic college hires only Catholic faculty. A Catholic does
what the pope tells him to do.

The Curialists have prepared an elaborate litany of Catholic identity.
Catholics, we are told, identify with life from its beginning to the very
end—no intervention in fertility, no birth control, no abortion, no homo-
sexuality, no euthanasia, no gay marriage. That is certainly a possible
paradigm of Catholic identity, but it falls apart empirically on the first
two criteria. Most Catholics do not think, as we shall see subsequently,
that either intervention in fertility or birth control is wrong. That's part
of the destabilization caused by the council and the leadership's failure
to implement the council.

Everyone seems interested these days in defining Catholic identity—
movements and Movements, RCIA and Neo-Catechumenate, liturgists
and "religious" educators, curial vigilantes and the rear-guard of "social
actionists." No one wonders how the Catholic laity defines their Catholic

Table 3.1
Components of Catholic Identity
(% very important)

Resurrection of Jesus	81%
Presence of God in the Sacraments	81%
Presence of Jesus in the Eucharist	75%
Concern for the poor	75%
Devotion to Mary the Mother of Jesus	75%
Daily prayer	63%
Emphasis on social justice	63%
Angels and saints	63%
Weekly Mass attendance	46%
Rejection of abortion	39%
Infallible pope	34%
Confession	30%
Celibate priesthood	24%

identity. Then Professor Dean Hoge of the Catholic University composed a list of twelve "elements" of Catholicism and asked how important each was (ranging from "very important" to "not too important at all"). The elements ran from "helping the poor" to "celibate male clergy" and included such matters as "devotion to Mary the Mother of Jesus" and "teachings in opposition to abortion."

The merit of this scale is that it permits respondents to choose those aspects of the Catholic heritage that are the most important to them, that tie them most deeply to the Church, that are the glue that holds everything else together, that they would never give up. The scale has been used in different forms and in different countries (Monsignor Conor Ward and I administered it in Ireland as part of the Irish participation in the International Social Survey Program). It is mostly invariant across demographic variables. While the percentages of respondents saying "very important" may differ in different contexts, the top five items in all the studies are the same.

In the present research more than three-fifths of the respondents said that helping the poor, the resurrection of Jesus from the dead, the presence of God in the Sacraments, presence of Jesus in the Eucharist, and Mary the Mother of Jesus were "very important." At the bottom of the list were abortion, teaching authority, death penalty, and celibate male clergy.

Who can fault an identity that inc
the resurrection, the Eucharist, and M
tity—those which are *really* importai
like The Annunciation, Christmas,
Easter. They are pictures but also n
the Upper Room, the Last Judgmer
Catholic Imagination (David Tracy's
material from which theology and
holds the community together, the a
roots of the rain forest that is the
within that forest for both Our Lae
option for the poor, Easter lilies, th
and much else besides.

The Catholic respondents knew
solutely essential in their religion—
Sacraments. After a couple thousan
get it "spot on" as our English col
achievement, especially in these ye
doesn't exist) and sexual abuse cri

There are other elements in the
portant. The point is the faithful a
people might say, "totally import
are enormous and indeed invincib
"evangelization" and they are ther
that religion starts with image ar
rules, however necessary these a

But Mary? Why Mary? Have v
theologians that she is an unfortur
about it! Any story that suggests
her new born child will never go
that image of God will never lo
mation of the world. No wonder
Guadalupe into their churches

The Church is in deep crisis
desperately needs reform (whe
has these powerful symbols,
Professor Hoge, recently emer
a tool that enables us to get in
and understand that fundamen
all the ages. If one could hire

identity q
from thos

The sa
communi
whatever
perfectly)

The da
includes c
Catholic I
to daily pr
which incl
Mass, infa
gested tha
commitme
gests a con
it suggests
Mary facto
The young
to embrace
values, perl
the discussi
powerful cc
ately endor

Howeve
esting corre
in the Sacra
also the imp
and the imp
likely to enc
celibate prie
and social ju

4

Cafeteria Catholicism

In 1976, I published a book called *The Communal Catholic* (Greeley, 1976) in which I suggested that there two kinds of Catholics had emerged in the years after the council—"Institutional Catholics," who obeyed or tried to obey all the rules and laws promulgated by the Church, and "Communal Catholics," who continued to attach themselves in some fashion to the Church, but now to the community of its members rather than to the rules laid down by those in Church authority. It seemed to me that in the wake of the study my colleagues and I had made of the changes in Catholic behaviors (Greeley et al., 1976) that some Catholics were making their own decisions on which Catholic rules (most notably the rule on birth control) they would obey and which they would reject. I did not defend such decisions but I argued that they were being made constantly and that Church leadership was only deceiving itself by denying that fact. I was accused of encouraging people to leave the Church, though perhaps only by those who had not read what I had written. It is not clear even today that many Catholic leaders are willing to acknowledge what was happening and what had happened. As I argued in *The Catholic Revolution* (2004a) the council led Catholics to expect change. The birth control encyclical was a bitter disappointment. They did not leave the Church; however, in overwhelming numbers they decided to become Catholics on their own terms. Those who disapproved of such behavior dismiss them as "Cafeteria Catholics," a term which is often used with contempt. But it is in the nature of Communal Catholics that they pay little attention to such condemnations. They are no longer listening, neither to the arguments nor to the denunciations. They can't be Catholics, I am told, if they behave that way. To which I try to reply that they think they can. They are wrong, I'm told. I note that one ceases to be a Catholic only if one formally abjures the faith or joins another denomination. We will have a smaller and stronger church, then, and we will be better for it. What if they won't go? I ask.

Again, I am not approving of such behavior. I am recording it and (trying to) challenge the leadership to listen to this communal. Without such willingness to listen on the part of the authorities (which many seem to think deprives them of their dignity) the destabilization will continue. Leaders and followers will live in different worlds and the Catholic institution and the Catholic community will be far apart. Table 4.1 shows just how powerful that destabilization is in Chicago.

The questions on which Table 4.1 is based are in effect about the outer boundaries of the Catholic community as defined by the laity. The Chicago respondents are not saying that they have failed in these matters or even that they approve of the behavior. They are merely asserting that they are not willing to expel from the community of the faithful, those who engage in the various activities.

Good Catholics, our respondents assert in overwhelming numbers, must believe in the resurrection of Jesus and his real presence in Eucharist. Solid majorities also contend that good Catholics give money to the poor and to the support of their parish. And a small majority also says that good Catholics have their marriages approved by the Church. For all the other items, only minorities of Chicago Catholics are willing to impose such obligations of those who wish to be considered (by the respondents) to be "good" Catholics. Only about a third agree that the good Catholic has to attend Mass every week and accept the Church's teaching on birth control and on abortion, on divorce and remarriage, and on the death penalty (higher than many would have expected); only a quarter believe that the "good" Catholic must accept the Church's teaching on immigrants and only one in twenty say that the good Catholic votes the way the bishops and the priests tell him to vote in elections. We will return to this conflict between identities subsequently.

There are ten "doctrines" on the list that are meant to be taken seriously (mortal sins in the old parlance), eight if one excludes immigrants and voting, and seven if one excludes war and peace. Only 7 percent of Chicago Catholics accept the five rules (abortion *and* birth control *and* divorce *and* infallibility *and* gay marriage) that constitute the "Life" Catholic identity of the curialists. If this is not "cafeteria" Catholicism, then what should it be called?

These findings may be a savage blow to those who want a smaller and holier church—it would include only 4 percent of the college graduates,

Table 4.1
Who is a Good Catholic?
(% yes)

Believes in resurrection of Jesus	94%
Believes Jesus is present in the Eucharist	92%
Donates money to help the poor	75%
Donates time and money to parish	66%
Has marriage approved by Church	54%
Accepts Church's teaching on war and peace	44%
Accepts teaching that abortion is always wrong	37%
Accepts teaching on divorce and remarriage	36%
Accepts Church's teaching on gay marriage	36%
Accepts Church's teaching on death penalty	33%
Believes pope is infallible	33%
Goes to Church every Sunday	32%
Obeys Church's teaching on birth control	30%
Accepts Church's teaching on divorce and remarriage	32%
Accepts Church's teaching on immigrants	24%
Votes the way bishops and priest suggest	5%

only 5 percent of those born since 1960, and 4 percent of the men (10 percent of the women). The percentages would doubtless be even smaller if artificial fertilization was included on the agenda.

The issue of war and peace is especially pertinent at the present time as the Iraq war continues. Forty-four percent of Chicago Catholics think that the Good Catholic must accept the church's teaching on war and peace—54 percent of those born since 1989, 49 percent of those who have graduated from college, and half of the women. For this issue of Church authority (not a matter of mortal sin) the young, the better educated, and the women Chicago Catholics are either on the pope's side or very close to it—which suggests that the official teaching on this issue is taken more seriously than it is on the other official teachings which are under discussion. If one constructs a scale of *zeal*—concern for social justice, concern for the poor, and concern for war and peace, 16 percent of the Chicago Catholic women and 16 percent of the college graduates can be considered to be *zealous*.

There is a long history of college-educated Catholics becoming active in social justice matters and staying with the cause through most of their lives. In the thirties and forties, Father Martin Carabine S.J. presided over a group called the Chicago Inner Scholastic Catholic Action (CISCA) out of which came many social activists, such as John Cogley and James O'Gara, who presided over *The Commonweal* magazine for many years. In subsequent years up to the time of the Vatican Council, priests like Reynold Hillenbrand, John Egan, William Quinn, and Water Imbiorksi and lay leaders like Patrick and Patricia Crowley were involved in lay movements like the Cana Conference, the Christian Family Movement, the Young Christian Workers, and the Young Christian Students and Edward Marciniak presided over the Catholic Labor Alliance. These men and women, God be good to them all, were among my mentors. It is consoling to speculate based on this finding that the spark may still be out there.

The findings are interesting. On war the Church leadership still has some credibility. On the other issues, their credibility seems to be fading away. The smaller, more obedient Church that conservative Catholics are calling for would be very small indeed, almost invisible. Perhaps Church leaders may need a more indirect approach to the young men and women who were not alive during the Vatican Council and have no memory of what it was like before destabilization. Save for those in the possession of ideological nostalgia, I don't think young people today would have liked it very much.

Insisting on the agenda contained in the "Life" identity is not likely to be successful. The absolute authority of the papacy disappeared in the first decade after the council, because the curialists thought it would be business as usual once the bishops were out of town. The implementation (particularly the birth control encyclical) imposed by the curia was botched and indeed only made the destabilization more acute. On the other hand, Catholic leaders can hardly be expected, for example, to change their teaching on abortion or gay marriage. Their conviction that the faithful are still listening to them is self-deceptive as well as self-serving. Moreover the "dissenters," which is practically everyone else, have made it clear that they like being Catholic and have no intention of leaving, perhaps not even if they are forced out. Authority may fume that the laity cannot do what the Chicago Catholic laity are doing and that they are poor Catholics. The laity does not so much disagree as they simply do not hear the fuming or do not take it seriously. And this phenomenon is worldwide. Chicago is but the green wood. How long can such dissidence continue without tearing the Church apart? It has persisted for almost forty years. The laity shows no sign of caving in. The leaders show no sign of recognizing their own responsibility for the catastrophic failures of the years after the council.

The laity would say in effect, hey, the Eucharist, the other Sacraments, the Resurrection, the poor, Mary—these are the core of our Catholic identity. You are going to throw us out because we are not incensed by gay marriages! And you didn't stop your priests from playing around with little boys! You gotta be kidding!

A sociologist does not argue with either side. He doesn't say the laity and the lower clergy are wrong. He says only that they are in dissent. Nor does he say that the leadership is wrong either. Only that their ineptitude in implementing the council turned a problematic situation into chaos—and then kept it there.

The only safe prediction seems to be that there will continue to be about 1.5 million Catholics in the archdiocese at mid-century (or maybe more depending on Mexican American immigration) and that there will be, whether the leadership likes it or not, varied forms of affiliation with a Church most of them still love. Not Cafeteria Catholics so much as Smorgasbord Catholics, a rich and diverse collection of ways to affirm one's Catholicism.

5

Time to Leave?

Jimmy Breslin remarked somewhere that the typical headline about Catholics in what he was pleased to call *The New York Times Newspaper* is "More Catholics Leaving Church than Ever." In much of the media coverage of the various crises in the Church in the last four decades, the assumption is the same as it was in the twenties and thirties of the centuries before last, the early days of American Nativism—the Catholic Church simply cannot survive in an open and democratic society. Public education will undermine the superstition of the Catholic faith, the Catholic population will break with its foreign leadership, the immigrants will become Americans, and Catholicism in the United States will become only a distant memory.

Each time a pope visited the United States in the last forty years some enterprising media outlet (and on some occasions, several such outlets) would do an article or a special program about the current Catholic crisis, which hinted at its conclusion that Catholics were increasingly fed up with their leadership (which was usually true) and that many, perhaps most of them (like the talking heads interviewed for the TV specials) seemed ready to leave. The surveys did not find, however, that large numbers were about to decamp.

Then when the next occasion for a survey came around the numbers were about the same. The big exodus had yet to occur. The sexual abuse crisis seemed to many the last straw. How could rational sensible people remain in such a Church—the assignment to answer that question was given to me by Jack Rosenthal, the then editor of *The New York Times Magazine*. My answer was that they stayed because they liked being Catholic and they liked the Catholic stories, responses which many Americans, particularly of the secularist variety, find no easier to get their heads around than did the Nativists of the early decades of the 19th Century.

In the present study, we asked the standard question, "How likely is it that you will leave the Catholic Church?" One and a half percent said it was "very likely," another 9.5 percent said "somewhat likely," and 20 percent said "not likely at all." These percentages do not differ greatly from previous surveys. Are they at odds with the 24 percent who said they had left the Church at some unspecified time in the past in chapter 2? Slight erosion over a lifetime, even of 1.5 percent can mount up over the years, but as of now there does not seem any greater propensity to decamp despite lay disgust over the sexual abuse mess. We posed a battery of explanations—sex abuse scandal, birth control teaching, insensitive priests, abortion teaching, too much change, Vatican Council, untrustworthy bishops, don't believe any more, obsession with money, spouse belongs to another Church, one Church is as good as another, another Church is more appealing, role of women in the Church. We then used a multiple regression equation to sort out the most powerful influences on the decision to think about leaving. When all the predictors were used in the equation, 20 percent of the variance was explained. The predictors with the strongest impact were the same ones that those who had already left reported—sex abuse, insensitive priests, untrustworthy bishops, birth control, abortion, insensitive priests, and role of women in the Church. When only these variables were left in the equation the variance explained fell to 12 percent and the strongest standardized correlations were four—bishops, priests, sex abuse, and abortion.

People think about leaving, including those who think that their departure is "not too likely" because of similar reasons for those who have already left—abused authority and sexual matters.

And why do they stay? We presented them with another cafeteria—you like being a Catholic, you've always been a Catholic, it is important to be part of the Catholic community, you have known many good priests, you still are attracted by the Catholic feasts and celebrations, it is important to pass on the tradition to your children, there is something special about being Catholic, you can't imagine not being Catholic, your spouse is Catholic and you go along...

When all these variables are poured into the multiple regression brew, they account for 34 percent of the variance in deciding to stay in the Church, a high-level explanation in the social science craft. You like being a Catholic, you've always been a Catholic, you value the Mass and the Sacraments, it's important to you to be part of the Catholic community, the ceremonies mean something to you, and the feasts and the celebrations are important to you. This curtailed list of reasons accounts for 32 percent of the variance. Leaving in only the strongest predictors—Mass and the Sacraments, Catholic community, and feasts and celebrations—still accounts for 30 percent of the variance, all telling one kind of a story or another. Catholics, I explained to Jack Rosenthal when I turned in my manuscript for the *New York Times Magazine*, is strong because it has the best stories. As I remember, they took a leaf from the Clinton Campaign of that time and headed the articles, "It's the stories, stupid!" Now I can prove it's the stories. Catholics remain Catholic, despite unsatisfactory leaders and monumental mistakes, because they love the Sacraments, the stories, and the community. All these variables are statistically significant by the standards of SPSS—.348, .219, and .160. If the leadership wishes to recapture its clout with the followers, they might keep that in mind.

6

Mass on Sundays

In the non-Latin world, Sunday Church attendance in the years before the Vatican Council was a major obligation, one the violation of
which was considered a grave, indeed, a mortal sin which, unless you
confessed it forthwith would provide you with a one way ticket to hell
for all eternity. Not only did one have to be present at Mass, but one
had to be present at the three main parts of the Mass under the same
penalty—Offertory, Consecration, and Communion (now called the
"Eucharistic Liturgy"). A Sunday golfer who sneaked out immediately
after the Lord's Prayer also merited a punch in his ticket to the neth-
erworld. Although a range of excusing reasons were available and one
was dispensed of the necessity of driving any more than a half hour to
find a Church, many Catholic travelers spared themselves no expense
of time or money in search of a Church. The priest might assure them of
the half hour dispensation and the dispensation that was provided by an
airplane trip before Sunday, but such dedicated Catholics insisted that
salvation was too important to accept any easy ways out.

One can locate the time of the change among the parish clergy and
the laity on birth control and of the change by the bishops of the Friday
abstinence rule, the de facto change on Sunday Mass is difficult to locate. Many Catholics availed themselves of the easy ways out that the
moral theologians had already offered—like a worn out mother needing
to sleep in (what mother does not need an occasional extra shut-eye?)
However, serious scholars of the sacraments discovered that the ruling
of the Council of Lateran about Sunday Mass was an attempt to persuade
the peasant converts from paganism that they ought to spend some time
in Church every week. That you would end up in hell if you didn't go to
Church was not a threat. It became a salutary warning perhaps in Ireland

during the Penal Years. Warnings about the hell fire that was waiting for you if you deliberately missed Mass on Sunday vanished from most Catholic teaching efforts during and after the council. The lower clergy were the ones who had legislated the changes in birth control and masturbation. The laity legislated the change in Sunday Mass. They had no authority to do that, you say? But they think they do. Indeed, in the current research 35 percent of Chicago Catholics cite that as a reason for not attending Church. Some theologians, most notably the Swiss Hans Kung, argued that Catholics ought to attend Mass every week not because the alternative was mortal sin and hell but because such attendance was a public evidence of their Catholic commitment and an encouragement to the commitment of others. You went to Mass on Sunday because it was a privilege and an honor to do so.[1] However, the change from damnation as motivation to generosity as motivation was not an easy one, especially when there was little in the Sunday liturgy to attract the faithful. Nationally the proportion of Catholics attending Sunday mass was 58 percent in 1964, 49 percent in 1974, and 33 percent in the early years of the new millennium—a decline of almost half in four decades. The attendance in Cook and Lake counties is somewhat higher—39 percent. Almost all of the national decline is accounted for by the change in cohorts, that is by younger generations (born after 1940, reaching adulthood during the council) who grow up with little sense of obligation to attend Sunday Mass and NOT by people who changed their behavior.[2] Thus, the challenge for the Church and its clergy is not to recall people to Sunday Church attendance (it is too late for that) but to invite a new generation to begin regular attendance for the first time. It will not be an easy task. But the alternative is a decline in weekly attendance to 15 percent (as table 6.1 shows.) All the October counts in the world will do nothing do stop the erosion.

Half of the respondents contend that they are too busy to attend weekly Mass (table 6.1) and more than two-fifths contend that they don't get anything out of Mass and the sermons are poor. A third protest the absence of a sense of mystery and a fifth that there is too much noise and that Mass takes too long. A regression equation that includes all the variables in Table 6.1 accounts for about half the variance in reasons for not attending weekly services, and only three variables account for 49 percent of the variance—poor sermons, don't get anything out of it, and that Mass is too long.

A typical clerical response to these complaints is that you are not supposed to get anything out of Mass. You are supposed to put something

Table 6.1
Reasons for Not Attending Weekly Mass
(% very or somewhat important)

Boring	35%
Work on Sunday	33%
Not a mortal sin	35%
Sermons are poor	44%
Don't get anything out of it	45%
It takes too long	22%
Too many people running around	9%
No sense of mystery	33%
Singing is terrible	12%
Can't pray there	9%
Too busy	52%
Too much noise	22%

into it, and do you mean you can't give an hour and fifteen minutes of your week to God? These responses miss the point. How can you put something into a ceremony that means little to you? And how can you become enthused about a ceremony that doesn't know how to end, but must extend itself through semi-literate or inarticulate comments from laity who add at least ten more minutes to the agony of boredom. Most of the laity shows up at Christmas and Easter because that's when the fires of the Catholic imagination are burning brightly, no thanks to the quality of the preaching. Why do they come only on Easter? Because those are the days they get something out of Mass.

A priest said to me recently that his congregation could not complain about preaching because the parish provided two excellent preachers. And the other two? Well, they know Father A works hard on his sermons and they love Fr. B because he visits the sick and goes to all the wakes. But effort on a sermon does not make it effective and while Father B does wonderful work with the sick and the bereaved that does not change the boredom of his homily. If the Church expects to increase the size of its Sunday congregations it has a lot of work to do on the quality of preaching and the quality of the Sunday liturgies—which would often mean taking Mass out of the hands of the liturgists. We are not supposed to be entertainers, complain the clergy. Yet, people followed after Jesus because they liked to listen to his stories.

While priests are blamed by those who left the Church and those who are thinking of leaving and at least implicitly blamed for the absence of a compelling liturgy, Chicago Catholics are generally sympathetic to their priests. Thus, when presented with a cafeteria of frequently heard anti-clerical comments about priests (table 6.2), majorities of Chicago Catholics reject most of them and complain only that they are in short supply (88 percent). Sixty-four percent protest that priests and nuns are rigid about rules. A little less than two out of five think that they are autocratic and don't understand what life is like for the laity. Twenty-nine percent think they won't share power with the laity, and twenty-six percent think they are not fair. Sixteen percent protest that priests and nuns don't have to earn a living, and thirteen percent say they are not available when you need them. By most classic measures of anticlericalism these reactions are very mild. Moreover, there are no significant correlations with age or gender or education with these attitudes. Most important nine-tenths of them say that the big problem with clergy types is that there are not enough of them which are in a way a high compliment. We have some problems with them, especially that they are often clueless, but please send us more.

Some would say ordaining women and married men (or permitting priests to marry) would solve these problems. Such remedies might indeed be a big help in responding to the laity's plea for "more." However, I must note here that the kind of priests that the laity currently have—celibate males—are the happiest men in the country (Greeley, 2004b), far happier than married Protestant clergy. The availability of the latter for their parishioners, as they admit, is limited by their responsibility to their families.

Table 6.2
Anticlerical Complaints about Priests and Nuns
(% Mentioning)

39%	Don't understand what life is like for laity
64%	Are rigid about rules
37%	Are autocratic
13%	Think they have all the answers
13%	Are not available when you need them
13%	Are not fair
26%	Don't have to earn a living
16%	Don't seem to have professional standards
29%	Won't share power with parishioners
88%	Are in too short supply

The final percentage in the table testifies how much respect remains for priests and nuns despite the problems the laity might have with them and despite the sex abuse crisis. They want more priests and nuns. It might help in this goal to let them know how much they are appreciated.

Notes

1. Later Father Roland Murphy, the distinguished Carmelite Biblical scholar who died too young, and I were boarding a bus that would take the participants of the meeting off to dinner. A very unusual colleague, typically French in appearance, was ahead of us. He turned on the top step and remarked, "le Pere Kung c'est tres pietist, non?"
2. These data are based on analysis of NORC's General Social Survey N=31, 222.

7

Priests at Work

In the fifties *Catholic Digest Magazine* commissioned Gallup to undertake a comparative study of American Catholics and Protestants and their clergy. Both rated their clergy highly, two-fifths of each denomination reporting that the sermons were "excellent." Unfortunately, the data were lost as were the cross-tabulation sheets. NORC asked similar questions on several different occasions, beginning with the first Catholic School Study (Greeley & Rossi, 1966) and subsequently in the General Social Survey. In the *Education of Catholic Americans*, the proportion of Catholics reporting "excellent" preachers had declined to 20 percent, where it has remained fixed for forty years, while Protestant preachers still won 40 percent of the votes. Not only were they less likely to claim excellent preaching, they were far less likely to endorse the preaching of priests that Protestants were likely to praise their clergy. In the absence of the data from the original Gallup study, it is difficult to explain this phenomenon. Had priestly preaching deteriorated that badly or had the increase in Catholic higher education raised their standards or perhaps there willingness to be blunt? Anyone who has listened to Catholic laity comment on preaching knows that the subject is likely to occasion brutal denunciation of the incompetence of the Sunday preachers. Somehow none of this unhappiness seems to have made it through rectory doors. One very rarely hears in conversation among priests that preaching may be a major ministerial problem for them. Quite the contrary, anyone who has a reputation for good preaching—calls to the rectory asking what Mass he will say—is likely to fall victim of the contumely of other priests as in, "yeah, he's a pretty good preacher, but he doesn't do much else and he's hell to live with."

There are a number of stories in table 7.1:

Table 7.1
Rating of Clergy's Work by Gender and Study
(% excellent)

	NORC* Protestants		Catholics		Chicago Men	Women
	Men	Women	Men	Women		
Preaching	28%	36%	18%	18%	29%	48%
Liturgy	29%	35%	25%	27%	42%	51%
Respect for Women	30%	39%	36%	33%	29%	42%
Sympathetic Counseling	36%	32%	32%	24%	52%	48%
Youth	29%	32%	21%	20%	49%	51%
Warmth			35%	47%		
Honesty			45%	53%		
Kindness			51%	57%		
Energy			37%	51%		
Friendliness			50%	50%		
Intelligence			41%	51%		

Source: General Social Survey

1. In the national sample, Protestant ministers continue to have a clear advantage over Catholic priests in preaching, counseling, worship, and youth work.
2. Nationally there is little variation across gender lines for Catholics.
3. Chicago Catholics rate their clergy much higher on all the items than do people in the national sample both Catholics and Protestants.
4. Chicago Catholic women rate their clergy higher than do Chicago Catholic men, save on counseling and friendliness.

Are Chicago priests that good or are Chicago laity that generous?[1]

Another series of items provides Chicago Catholics with an opportunity to list important services that they expect a Church to provide for them and their families and then to evaluate how their local parish is responding to these perceived needs. It is unlikely that the respondents had ever considered these issues explicitly before they received the call from the Survey Lab. They had to make quick decisions about the relative importance of such matters as marriage, parents, children, life, and death. Then they had to make quick judgments about how their local parish responded to these situations. In table 7.2, the first column describes the human situation that requires a response, the second lists the proportion of Chicago Catholics who consider the problem "very important" while the third column indicates what proportion of Chicago Catholics thought that the response of the local parish was "excellent." Lastly, the final column describes the difference between the proportion who thought the issue was extremely important and the proportion that judged the response was "excellent."

Some priests, this one included, would consider the agenda of human needs to be daunting. How can we possibly be skilled in all those life situations—the death of a spouse or a child, a crisis in a marriage, for example? In fact, if one adds the proportion that describes a response as "good" to the proportion saying it was "excellent," the percentage in the last column diminishes and sometimes disappears. However, "very important" was the first possible response to the question about the desire of a response from the Church and "excellent" was the first possible response to the question about the quality of response. Does not a Catholic layperson (in Chicago or anywhere else) have a right to an excellent response to questions about keeping a marriage together, about death, about children, and about faith? The laity does not necessarily expect perfection from us. But do not they have a right to a good answer to these kinds of anxieties? Why else do they pay for our education, feed us, provide us with cars, and enable us to live in a comfortable lifestyle if we do not have first-rate answers to these fundamental life situations?

It does not seem unfair, therefore, to conclude that table 7.1 suggests that they would like it if we could cope with life crises with more ingenuity, insight, sensitivity, and faith than they normally encounter. On the other hand, it is also my experience after I have made a mess in dealing with one of those marital problems that the patent gratitude of the couple indicates that even an inept priest can make do when he does his best to help—which is no excuse for not trying to improve.

I also note that the Chicago laity think in table 7.1 that their priests work well with young people and that there is no God given dispensation to avoid the young, especially since they seem (in the next chapter) to be impressive men and women.

One might therefore conclude from tables 6.2, 7.1, and 7.2 that the laity are reasonably satisfied with the efforts of their priests and stoutly defend them, but their loyalty does not prevent them from wishing that sometimes our performance in crises situations was better than it is.

Table 7.2
Church Work That Is Important to Laity and the Church's Response

	% "Very Important"	% Local Church's Response "Excellent"	Difference
Meaning and purpose of life	71%	40%	-31%
Community to belong to	72%	40%	-32%
Help in holding a marriage together	63%	26%	-37%
Help in religious education of children	84%	47%	-37%
Help with elderly parents	63%	26%	-37%
Hope in times of trial and difficulty	77%	39%	-38%
Faith in God who loves you	83%	48%	-35%
A heritage to pass on	71%	35%	-36%
Values to which to commit	71%	32%	-39%
Consolation at death of loved ones	81%	47%	-34%
Preparation for your own death	54%	29%	-25%
Awareness of spiritual dimension of life	64%	31%	-33%
More understanding of the mysteries of God	62%	27%	-35%

Note

1. The same findings—high ratings for Chicago priests by their laity and higher still by women—were found in the pretest. Thus, if the ratings seem too high it is not a function of the data collection by the Survey Lab.

8

Secularized Young People

Table 8.1
Secularization and Young Chicago Catholics

	Correlation with Youth (born after 1972)	% Agree	Correlation with Graduate Degree
Mary	.07	62%	-.25
Attends several times a month	.24	49%	.06
Pray every day	.18	41%	.09
Wont leave	.09	72%	.04
Catholic faith Important	.10	81%	-.18
Life after death	.13	88%	.06
A Good Catholic Should			
Believe in Resurrection	.05	94%	.11
Believe in Eucharist	.11	91%	.05
Agree on Death Penalty	-.15		-.11
Accept Birth Control teaching	-.24	23%	-.15
Accept abortion teaching	-.09	34%	-.07
Accept immigration teaching	-.08	23%	.13
Pope is infallible	-.21	32%	.12
Accept teaching on war	-.09	44%	.xx
Accept teaching on gay marriage	-.12	28%	.12
Cohort Youngest		Degree (graduate school)	
32%	.12	49%	-.22

In an article filed from a meeting of Catholic bishops, perhaps of the committee responsible for media relations, John Allen the perceptive international correspondent of the *National Catholic Reporter* detailed the sentiments of the Lord's Spiritual on young Catholics. The problem they agreed was that the young were victims of "secularization." Exactly what this shibboleth means is difficult to specify, though on the lips of bishop it is always bad, almost always something for which they are not responsible, frequently is the fault of the laity, permeates the air like a swampy miasma, and must be confronted by stern warnings from the Magisterium (by which they mean[1] themselves) and strict enforcement of all pertinent rules. Minimally it means that young people generally aren't as virtuous as they used to be and that they are obsessed by sex. Obedience to the Magisterium and control of passion in a world dense with temptations are minimally required behavior for those seeking to be "practicing" Catholics.

Given the strong reproductive urge of species *Homo,* it seems problematic that humankind is more obsessed by sex than it ever was. Nor is there evidence available that contemporary humankind is less inclined to forego sexual pleasure that it has ever been. The golden age of sexual abstinence is, like all other golden ages, mostly mythical. What may have changed is the willingness of the young to accept authority that claims the right to prescribe for the young what is appropriate sexual behavior. What may have changed is the willingness of older people to dictate when non-marital sex is morally wrong for their contemporaries.

Among social sciences "secularization" applies not merely to sex. Rather it predicts the decline of religion because of the social changes which have occurred since the Reformation, mostly through the use of terms over which the aura of science has been cast by the use of the "letters IZ" in the middle of a word. Thus, secularIZation is the result of modernIZation, rationalIZation, and urbanIZation. It is the result of scientific progress, the enlightenment, and the decline of superstition and belief in magic. Humankind no longer needs God or religion or a Church. This notion was first advanced in America not by scientists but by social scientists and humanists, many of them children of clergy or even clergy themselves. Forty years ago, there was no American data available to confirm that this evolution of the humankind away from the "God hypothesis," but theologians took it for granted that religion was in decline. Then the national surveys began to emerge and while some of the survey takers searched intensively for signs of religious decline, they were not successful. They then began to argue that either this was a case of American exceptionalism because the US had yet to catch up with Europe or that American respondents were not answering honestly. East German sociologists studying the former Socialist country explained away the apparent religious revivals in such countries as Poland as evidence that they had yet to "modernize." When they did "modernize," secularization would take effect. Heads we win, tails you lose.

No evidence, in other words, could be permitted to change the conventional wisdom. In the United States, there was considerable discussion about what secularization really meant. Mark Chaves (1993) has offered a solution: secularization means that religious authority, all religious authority, has lost the power to command automatic assent from its members. It cannot impact their behavior (voting, drinking) or their convictions (death penalty, birth control).

Yet somehow Professor Chaves' "compromise" has nothing to offer those scholars who argue that religion is no longer as important as it used to be. The human impulse to believe persists (note that in the subsequent personal interviews chapter those who have left the Church continue to believe in God) despite the predictions of so many scholars from Voltaire to Hitchins, God seems to be alive and well as an object of belief. Professor Charles Thomas, a Canadian historian and philosopher, sees many phases in the emergence of a "secularized life," the first of which is a demystification of life. The forests are no longer the hiding place for fairies, ghosts do not live in haunted rectories, and spirits do not hover around cemeteries. The dead do not reappear on All Hallows Eve. Might, on rare occasions, the membrane separating the Church triumphant (or suffering) from us be temporarily permeable? Perhaps the deluge of ghost programs on TV is a fad.

The sociologist notes the absence of data. Are Chicago Catholics, living as they do, in a rain forest of sacraments, open to the possibility of signs and wonders. Again, the sociologist awaits the arrival of better data, but does not expect any to show up tomorrow morning in a Federal Express package.

These issues are beyond the concern of most bishops. They are more interested in a one-word explanation that will account for the decline of their credibility. Few will stand up and say bluntly, "We messed up." Hence, they have a vested interest in "secularization" as a reality. Since secularization assumes progress, it should be more common among those who are younger, those who represent the future, and among those with more education and hence are more interested in the modernization that change may have brought.

Hence, studying the data collected in the "Chicago Catholic" we can ask whether the data in the study are compatible with a decline of a sense of the sacred among younger and better-educated Chicagoans? Are they less likely, for example, to take seriously Mary the Mother of Jesus and the Angels and Saints? Are they also less likely to accept the official teachings of the Magisterium on sexuality—or anything else? There is no straightforward answer to these questions. The younger cohort of the Chicago sample are, however, if anything more "mystified" than Professor Charles might expect and substantially less likely to be the docile peasants that some Church leaders in Europe thought they encounter before the "War." Faith persists, obedience does not.

They are more likely to emphasize devotion to the mother of Jesus, the Presence of Jesus in the Eucharist, the resurrection, the presence of God in the Sacraments, to attend Mass frequently, and to pray every day. They also are more likely to be active in their parishes.

One must ask how much the bishops at the meeting where Mr. Allen heard some of the best minds of the American hierarchy write off the younger cohorts had done much to stay in contact with the presumably pagan youth of their faithful. How much activity among teens and young adults is to be found in the contemporary Catholic Church? Christian Smith of the University of North Carolina at Chapel Hill and now of the University of Our Lady of the Lake (AKA Notre Dame) reports (Smith and Emerson, 2008) that the Catholic Church is less likely than any of the other denominations to invest funds for personnel in youth work. He also reports that the Catholic young people he has encountered display high levels of enthusiasm for their Church. It is unlikely that any of the bishops at the conference (in Orlando) have read Professor Smith's book. Bishops do not have to read sociology to qualify as experts.

The High Clubs and the Teen Clubs of yesteryear seem to have vanished. The sexual abuse crisis, I am told, makes such encounters unwise.[2] The accompanying Table 8.1 illustrates the findings. The first column illustrates the attitudes and behavior of young Catholics. A positive correlation indicates that the younger Catholics are *more* likely than older Catholics to endorse the propositions while a negative correlation indicates that younger Catholics are less likely to accept the proposition than are older Catholics.

Thus, younger Catholics are more likely to believe in the importance of the mother of Jesus, the presence of Jesus in the Eucharist, the resurrection and to assert that their Catholic faith is very important to them and that they are most unlikely to leave the Church and are more likely to attend Mass frequently and to pray daily. On these matters of religious imagery, devotion, and faith, we can find no evidence that is compatible with religious decline. The respondents in the millennial cohort (born after 1972) are apparently more "active" in their Catholicism than are their parents and grandparents. Forty-one percent (the proportion in the second column) of all Catholics pray at least once a day, younger Catholics pray even more frequently (r=.18). The bishops at the Orlando meeting may say that it is not that way in their dioceses. They may well be correct in that estimate, but they are in effect admitting that Catholic faith, devotion, and practice are stronger in Chicago than they are in their own dioceses. However, the remaining items in the first column, which measure acceptance of the Church's moral teachings, present a different view. Older Catholics are more willing to accept the Church's perspective about the relative difference on the Church's right to teach on moral matters such as birth control, abortion, the death penalty, the infallibility of pope, gay marriage, immigration, and war and peace. Indeed, while the younger Catholics are more likely to reject these teachings than their predecessors are, a minority of the whole sample seems to accept only a narrow interpretation of what Catholic doctrine requires on these issues. Indeed two-thirds of all the respondents (and more so the younger ones) rejects all Church authority on these matters.

Thus, there seems to be ambiguity among Chicago Catholics on the issues in the first column. Younger Catholics are more in tune with basic doctrines of faith and devotion than older Catholics and to have on these issues stronger convictions than do older Catholics. On the other hand, in matters of what might be called issues of morality and especially sexual morality the younger seem less moral than the older. The second half of the first column thus substantiates the view of the Orlando meeting of Catholic bishops that the younger are more secularized than the older and supports Mark Chaves' perspective on secularization.

One might be temped to tease the bishops—if you absolutely had to choose would you rather have young people who believe in the Real Presence and in life after death or those who reject gay marriages and birth control?

The fact that Catholics sharply distinguish the moral "rules" in Catholicism from the Catholic faith (as they define it) is not new. Since the early studies after the council (Greeley 1966; Greeley, McCready, and McCourt, 1976) this finding as been repeated so often that the leadership of the Church has tried to impugn the finding and to claim that there is evidence (in the devotion at the World Days of Youth or at the conclaves) that the Catholic faith is as strong as it ever was. In the present analysis no claim is made that enthusiasm for the faith is incompatible (de facto though not necessarily de jure) with laity making their moral decisions independent of the rules laid down by the magisterium. This independence is so evident four decades after the council that only ignorance or intellectual dishonesty could account for it. Catholic laity will make their own decisions on moral matters, especially when the subject is marital sex, but also matters like immigration and the death penalty. The bright optimism of Church leadership during the past forty years is not justified by the facts. The teaching Church and the believing Church are separated on this issue and have been since the 1968 birth control encyclical. It is not the proper role of the sociologist to say how this situation might change. However, despite all the insistence, the warnings, and the citations in the Catechism, there is no sign of a return to the status quo ante.

The current study, as much as it may be condemned for reporting statistical facts, is hardly necessary to repeat previous findings. However, the more intriguing phenomena is that on issues of faith (resurrection and Eucharist), devotion (Mass and payer), and religious imagery (Mary and Sacraments) the youngest cohort seems more strongly Catholic than its predecessors—perhaps because it is more at ease with the practice of being Catholic on their own terms.

I note here for the record that I am saying it is right proper for them to do that. I am rather insisting that young Catholics do not look to the magisterium for guidance in such matters and now seem so untroubled by this "cafeteria" Catholicism as to become more Catholic (in, for example, the many enthusiastic volunteer movements).

A final question is whether graduate school education leads to a "secularization" phenomenon. The fourth column in the table shows that graduate school education leads to a decline in both devotional and imaginative Catholicism among younger Catholics. Those young Catholics who have attended graduate school are in fact significantly lower on the indicators that indicated change among younger Catholics. This finding causes problems because younger Catholics are likely to have more graduate school experience than do older Catholics. Do youthfulness and education tend to cancel out secularization among young people?

Michael Hout (private correspondence) reports: "In the GSS the proportions of BAs and the grad school folks staying in Church are not significantly different in any cohort. They show a 25-point drop from

1910's to 1950's and a slight rebound (6 percentage points) for the 1960's and 1970's birth cohorts."

The data from the General Social Survey are national and, hence, suggest that national data about young people are compatible with those observed in Chicago and that graduate school has no effect beyond that of college education on religious behavior. In fact, the curves of belief in life after death by birth cohort in the General Social Survey data in this research are similar. The question is why there was a decline in religiousness among those who were born in the early decades of the century and then a rebound among the more recent cohorts. Indeed, in an article Professor Hout and I published (Hout and Greeley) we demonstrated a sharp increase in belief in life after death during the 20th Century, mostly because of an increase in such belief among Catholics, Jews, and those with no religious faith, especially among Catholics.

At first, such a phenomenon seemed most unlikely (not to say counter-intuitive). The Catholic immigrants were moving from a rural to an urban society, from an informal culture to a formal one, from an agricultural way of life to an industrial one. They were being rationallZed with a vengeance. Certainly, their religious faith ought to erode under all those pressures. The very title of the classic book about this migration, *The Polish Peasant in Europe and America,* suggested that the peasant religion would be hard pressed to simply maintain its power over the lives of its followers. To increase their doctrinal orthodoxy would suggest perhaps that shamans of some sort were engaging in witchcraft. Yet, in a couple of generations, peasant immigrants were becoming more and more Catholic in their orthodoxy. The vague instinct of my immediate ancestors to believe that the grave was in some sense the permanent residence of their loved ones was what peasants might believe. Yet an increase in belief in life after death across 20th Century cohorts was so improbable that some of the readers of our article express serious doubts.

Professor Hout and I speculated that the final waves of late 19th-Century immigration were, especially if they were eastern or southern Europe folk Catholics, strongly committed to their faith but unsophisticated in the details of that faith. In a country where the Protestant host culture of the time accepted the notion of human survival, the Catholic leadership was in a position to use the funeral practices of Americans (which included wakes) as a model for teaching its own formal doctrines. The Catholic Church, now much better organized for the immigrants than it had been in the years after the Famine, could devote its resources—institutional and human—to socializing them into a Catholicism that strove to be both

Catholic and American. In the big cities like Philadelphia, New York, and Chicago the Catholic schools would dismiss as superstitious massive family visits to cemeteries on birthdays, anniversaries, and patron saints days. By the end of the 20th Century, American Catholics had a pretty good idea what they absolutely had to believe. The wakes continued, though they were more restrained than in the old country and later generations came to believe that one night was enough for a wake.[3]

The belief that humans survive death is vivid and consoling. The transformation of the immigrants into people who embraced, to a greater or lesser extent the hopefulness of the analogical imagination created a religious background in which younger Catholics could make decisions about what you had to believe and what you *really* had to believe, between what the Church demanded and what God expected. The Catholic Church had succeeded in defending the faith of the confused immigrants. It has had a much more difficult time in responding to the confusion created by the Vatican Council. But there were no theories about how to respond to a seismic change. Denial of the fact of the change just didn't work. The rigid structures of the immigrant Church until about 1960 worked very well. The same structures, administered often by the same men, were catastrophic failures in the years after the council. So the laity, having sought education as they had been taught by their leaders, began to make their own decisions.

The leaders insisted that they could not do that. Some of them seem to believe that their firmness prevented chaos and that all is well. Look at the great devotion to John Paul II. Look at the enthusiasm of the World Day of Youth Ritual!

It might be very interesting to do a survey before the next world youth day and then another one after it—like my colleagues did (by chance) before and after the council. But that would be to question the impact of the Holy Spirit, would it not?

Will the present situation last? Will the internal conflict in the Church eventually destroy the American Catholic experiment? The Chicago Catholic experiment? The only answer seems to be that it hasn't done so in the last four decades. The narrative and symbolic Catholic rainforest of images still seems resilient.

Notes

1. Current research (Greeley, Greeley, and Hout).
2. When, in the Spring of 1954, I was assigned responsibility for the teens of the parish I was utterly unqualified. I had never been a teen. I had lost contact with my grammar school classmates. I couldn't have been more naïve. But I did know

that whenever there was a gathering of them on parish premises or parish projects, one should have at least a half dozen chaperones involved. I also knew that on one of my first nights in the parish, I should walk up to the corner drug store and that, despite my utter lack of skills, I should show up on the basketball courts. In those days, I thought that such knowledge came with oils of ordination. I left the parish ten years later with the feeling that I had failed the teenagers. Whether it was my fault is open to question.

3.   On the day of my father's burial, when the undertaker suggested that my mother and my siblings might want a "little privacy" to make our final farewells, we declined. "He's not in that casket," one of my sisters insisted. Over a single generation the socialization of the Irish emigrants on life after death had done its work.

9

Why Do They Stay?

Table 9.1
What Keeps Chicago Catholics in the Church?

	Men	Women
Explicit motives	.058	.220
Religion of spouse	-1.066	.014
Catholic imagination	.489	.079
Attended Catholic schools	.328	.241
Kids in Catholic schools	.038	xx
Children raised Catholic	.597	.587
Catholic friends	.238	xx
Like/ approve clergy professionalism	.155	.256
Responsiveness of parish to	.143	.102
Active in parish	.238	.630
Approve of pastor	.020	.143
Approve of Cardinal	.001	.005
R	.974	.820
R Square	.779	. 640

In a previous chapter we asked why Catholics stay in their church. The answer was provided by a factor created out of a number of responses that tightly intercorrelated with one another and seemed almost to scream in response, "we like being Catholic!" a cry that well seemed as improbable to many readers as my initial reply to Jack Rosenthal's question when he commissioned my article in the magazine. How can this be with the controversies currently raging among individual Catholics, between the Roman curia and much of the rest of the Church, and the nastiness and folly of the behavior of some of the Church's leaders? The answer I gave in that NYT article (Greeley, 1994) still stands—"because they like the stories!" With data available in this project I can perhaps essay a more detailed explanation: The Catholic stories interact with experiences of daily life—the stories are shared with spouse and children, attendance at Catholic schools of both parent and child, the appeal of the Catholic imagination, involvement in parish activities, membership in Catholic friendship groups, and approval of professionalism of clergy. (table 9.1)[1] The complex interaction of these influences and the stories about these influences are part of the glue that holds the Church together. In the battle between the Catholic heritage and other, seemingly more attractive and rational worldviews, for Catholics the playing field seems to be tilted.

Images, relationships, and experiences all contribute to the tilt. As your man from Dublin wrote, "Catholicism means here comes everyone!" from the Mother of Jesus to the effective parish priest. In a possible but unlikely comparative study between Chicago, and let us say, Philadelphia, it would be interesting to learn whether the constraints to remain Catholic are as strong as they are in Chicago.

Note

1.   The two columns of figures in table 9.1 are the result of a multiple regression equation, which estimates the influence of a variable on loyalty to the church net of all the other variables in the equation—thus the influence of parish activity net of all the other variables. The large regression coefficients at the bottom of the columns is an estimate of the combined influence of all the variables combined Thus we conclude that the model expressed by the table is a powerful explanation of why Catholics remain Catholic.

Ideally, it should be possible to create an elaborate path diagram showing the relationship of each variable with every other variable in the model. However that would have required data from many previous years to, let us say, show the additional contribution of, let us say, another child to the family. Because of lack of time and money, the goal of this model is to merely demonstrate that different influences cooperate in different ways for men and for women *and* that, in addition the stories and the imagery and the general loyalty to Catholic Catholicism the various relationships with both the institution and one's family contribute to a very powerful motivation for continuing to be a Catholic.

10

Competing Identities

In the chapter on Catholic identity we saw that there seem to be two separate Catholic identities—an imaginative, story-telling identity and a rules identity. More Catholics find their identity in the resurrection, the Eucharist, the Sacraments, the poor, and the Mother of Jesus than in support for the Church's teachings on abortion, birth control, gay marriages, and infallibility. A strict comparison between the two is not possible, because the "rules" ask what a good Catholic believes is proper in cases of abortion, birth control, gay marriage, divorce, and infallibility while the imaginative identity asks what stories are "very important" for their own personal Catholic identity. Both, however, are essential to the Catholic legacy. Moreover, there is some overlap on the two scales—they correlate with an R of .65, which means that approximately half of the variance on one scale can account for the variance on the other scale. They do not contradict one another. However, if one asks about the relative impact on remaining in the Church, the beta correlations are -.17 for the rules and -.43 for the stories and the betas for concern about social justice are .09. and .27, and for frequent prayer, .10 and .30. By any measure, the religious image identity is the more powerful of the two but neither loses their absolute importance when compared to the other. Nor is it surprising that images are more powerful than rules, Eucharist, resurrection, and Mary are more powerful than birth control and gay marriage rules. Neither is unimportant and both are part of the Catholic heritage. The critical point is that religious imagination and stories seem to be more fundamental than rules about sexuality, and the Church loses nothing by emphasizing the former. Catholicism is a both/and worldview. Yet, the images and stories are more powerful for keeping a Catholic in the Church and orienting a Catholic towards social justice and frequent prayer.

Ethnic Groups and Regions of the City

Table 11.1
Religious Profiles of Chicago Ethnic Groups
(coefficients in dummy variable multiple regression analysis)

	Irish	German	Italian	Polish	Eastern European	Hispanic
Education	.10					-.18
Age	.08			.11		-.14
Leave Church						
Imagination identity	.15					.13
Life identity				.15		
Professional clergy	.12			.14		
Responsive parish						.11
Active in parish	.11					
Pray						.10
Attend	.12			.15		.14
Life after death						
Spouse Catholic	.10	.10		.14		.11
5, Best friends Catholic						.13

It is very difficult to estimate cultural differences among Ethnic Groups and neighborhood communities within the Archdiocese. Even with more than 500 respondents, there are enough diverse ethnic groups that case bases quickly disappear. Moreover, men and women often marry beyond the boundaries of their ethnic origins so that many have some difficulty in determining what their ethnic background is. Approximately 41 percent say that they are "other" or "mixed." ("Irish" was the most frequent choice of a non-Irish spouse in the parental generation of our respondents). Other research indicates that those born of an ethnically mixed marriage usually choose the ethnic background of their father. Why does that not surprise anyone?

It seemed to be that ethnic variety is too important for Chicago Catholics to be ignored because of such problems and that therefore we would analyze the responses of those who told us their ethnic identification without complicating the matter into unintelligibility by inviting into the party too many ancestors. Thus, we will test a very general null hypothesis—there is not much diversity among Catholic ethnic groups in Chicago, the kind of opinion that migrants into the metropolitan area might form in a snap judgment if they have settled in an exclusive suburb. We will use a technique called "dummy" variable multiple regression, which enables us to determine whether there is statistically significant difference between the given ethnic group and all the other groups. The coefficients that are higher than .10—all statistically significant—are presented in table 11.1. The three groups that are different are the Irish, the Polish, and the Hispanic. The Irish were the earliest immigrants to Chicago and the Hispanics were the most recent. They are also the most likely to be different. The Irish and the Hispanics—the oldest and the most recent immigrants—are also the most distinctive, the Irish on educational attainment and age, the religious imagination identity, respect for the professional standards of the clergy, activity in the parish, belief in life after death, Church attendance, and a Catholic spouse. The Hispanics were lower on age and education, to be expected from recent immigrants and significantly higher on religious imagination, a responsive parish, prayer, Church attendance, a Catholic spouse, and best friends Catholic. The Poles were younger, emphasize life issues more than imaginative issues, were more likely to have Catholic spouses and to attend Mass frequently, and to respect the professionalism of their clergy. The Germans were distinctive in their propensity to choose Catholic spouses and there were no significant relationships with specific Catholic cultural matters for the Italians and the Eastern Europeans (Slovak, Slovene, Ukrainian, Hungarian, etc.).

From this convergence of specifically ethnic religious subcultures, one might hazard the expectation that the major Catholic ethnic groups had much in common but also enough diversity that the religious leadership ought to take the differences seriously. The Poles and the Hispanics share many neighborhoods in the city and seem to get along reasonably well together. Neither the Poles nor the Hispanics, however, are content with the power of Irish religious leadership. The Irish are, by history and personality, masters of the political game. They have governed both the city and the Church for a century though they do not dominate the city, much less the Church by their numbers. It would probably be useful for the mostly Irish ecclesiastical elite to be wary of edginess of the Poles and the energy of the Hispanics. One might even suggest that there be parades through the Catholic rainforest of symbols that appeal to all the ethnic groups by celebrating the unity and diversity that the rainforest revels.

My null hypothesis for the second section of this chapter is that region has no impact on community structure among Chicago Catholics. If it turns out that the null hypothesis cannot be supported, than the theory of the South Side is still open to examination. Perhaps one could investigate the possibility that the West Side culture moved into the western suburbs and the South Side culture still survives in the southern suburbs (and if one cares about the North Side) the North Side suburbs carries a distinct North Side taint or, if you will, flavor.

A problem arises immediately. There is little left of the West Side. Resegregation of the West Side parishes during the sixties and seventies leave few Catholic parishes and few Catholic neighborhoods beyond the boundary between Chicago and suburbs marked by the tall wall of Austin Boulevard. There survive only Oak Park, River Forest, Oak Brook, and such places that are not at all like the neighborhood where I grew up.

However, my own family, like so many others, migrated not to Oak Park or River Forest (too Protestant and too Italian) but to the northwest segment of the city and then to the less demonstrative suburbs like Norwich, Park Ridge, Mount Prospect, Des Plaines, and even Skokie. In such locales, West Side culture could still flourish and not be swallowed up by the Thorstein Veblenism of Evanston, Wilmette, Winnetka, Wauconda, Half Day, Mundelein, and so on.

Two hypotheses are up for examination: Are South Side Catholics (Irish or whatever) more likely to report that their five closest friends are Catholic than the West Siders? Are both more likely to feel that the friendship group rates are higher than the pathetic North Siders? There remains the problem of how the boundaries of these enclaves are to be defined. The North Side runs from the main branch of the river north to the city limits and from the north branch of the river to the lake. The South Side runs from the south branch of the river to the city limits and back to the lake. The Northwest Side runs from the north branch of the river to the city limits, including O'Hare International Airport.

Table 11.2
Catholic Friendship Groups by Region and Suburb
(% all close friends Catholic)

	All Close Friends Catholic		At Least Three Close Friends from Same Parish	
	Chicago	Suburbs	Chicago	Suburbs
North	28%	21%	13%	15%
North West	43%	61%	26%	15%
South	62%	51%	22%	32%

There are many theories about why Chicago Catholics tend to divide themselves along the lines of political theology, with South Side struggling always for supremacy over the West Side and never quite making it—even when the White Sox, through some astral magic, managed to win the World Series in four games. One thesis concerns the Irish who settled in the South Side (around Nativity Parish in Bridgeport were more militant in their nationalism) and lived in the shanties along the south bank of the river. They were probably wild on arrival from the bogs of Mayo and the enervating work on the canals made them even wilder. They were shanty Irish to begin with, this theory holds, and became even more shanty when they moved into the shanties and the cottages near the south bank of the river and went to work in the steel mills, which once lined the river and then the "Yards." How could you possibly be sensible and reasonable all the time when the stench of the slaughter permeated your homes, your churches, your schools, even your bedrooms? On the West Side, the Yards tormented us only on hot and humid summer nights. Moreover, the parishes "out there" were commanded by Irish born secular clergy who were directing their people to Irish nationalist causes.

On the West Side, we felt that we were civilized, refined, and well mannered. The Jesuits at Holy Family Parish strove to protect us from the gross behavior of our cousins south of 22nd Street. We thought, because our mothers told us so, that lace curtains on our windows were a sign that we were already one step away from the shanties, as we later would feel about our Venetian blinds, our picture windows, and our country clubs. The Jesuit fathers at Holy Family believed that our challenge was not to free Ireland from the English but to free ourselves from the bad manners of the rough neck folk who lived in the shanties.

That lovely and all-explaining theory seemed to fit the data and the gross reaction from our relatives who were condemned forever to be South Side Shanty Irish. I found them loud and vulgar and prided myself on dismissing them as not worthy of my attention (a stance hard to maintain when they won that four-game World Series) and dismissed their attempts to insist on their superiority as just part of a silly game that they liked to play.

I had perfected this stance in my seminary years while fending off nasty and unpleasant South Side classmates, nice enough young men, but always looking for a fight. Vulgar.

When I was assigned to my first parish at 92nd and Western, my good mother said in horror, "Is that on the South Side!" I admitted that it was. Did I believe any of this stuff? Of course not!

Moreover, our Black brothers and sisters had a South Side/West Side folk theory, except it was just the opposite of ours. It was a legend, like ours, a myth, and an urban legend that the South Siders fabricated to make up for their feelings of inferiority. As I have said many times in public print, they have much to feel inferior about. Like the stock yards smell.

I would repeat this mega theory often for my students both at the University of Arizona and at the University of Chicago: the South Side is uncivilized and vulgar, the West Side is refined and polite. And the North Side doesn't exist!

My Cardinal, who is from the West Side enjoys the game, so I'm home free.

Having indulged in all this delightful put down of friends and relatives, I must put my sociologist hat back on and wonder if regions can create durable subcultures. Is there a possibility that regional variation, as widely if thinly accepted, provides testable hypotheses? Can the geography and history of segments of a metropolitan area shape political and religious culture? I would be a poor sociologist if I did not, with a moderately open mind, explore that possibility?

I begin with a simple hypothesis that those of us who went through the Jesuit dominated, Americanist Holy Family Parish system; with its five grammar schools, two high schools, one college, and eventually a university; be a bit less clannish than those who went through Nativity, the Yards, and Comisky Park?

The first hypothesis is examined in the second column of table 11.2. There can be no doubt about the finding. The South Siders are more likely to be communal (as they would say) or clannish as we would say.

Forty-three percent of us say that our best friends are all Catholic and 62 percent of them say the same thing. A trivial 28 percent of those in the North Side—Lincoln Park, Edgewater, Lincoln Square, and Andersonville assert that their best friends are all Catholic. Sic Stat Thesis.

But, not so fast, Louie, in the three Suburban regions the North Siders are less likely to be communal (21 percent), the West Siders are more likely to be communal (51 percent), moving ahead of the South Side Suburbanites—Alsip Evergreen Park, Mount Greenwood (46 percent). Did we become more clannish when we moved to the suburbs?

The West Side wins the contest of whether three of the closest friends are from the same parish (present or past) in the third column of table 11.1. Twenty-six percent of those who live in the North West side of city report that their friends are from the same parish as opposed to 13 percent of the North West side city dweller and 22 percent of the South Side urbanite. In the Southwest suburbs the communalism prize goes to the South Side, where a third of the suburbanites say that at least three of their friends are from the same parish. Perhaps the reason for this is that so many of South Side Catholics moved out of the city at the same time when panic peddling swept wide swaths of South Side parishes and many of them ended up in the same refuge.

The two conclusions of this chapter are not trivial. At a time when Catholic liberals assert that white ethnicity is unimportant and want to lump all of us into the residual category of "European Americans," it is useful to be reminded that in large cities there still exist major ethnic groups (Warner, 2005) and diverse Catholic ethnic groups which must be treated with respect and concern (as the interviews in appendix C confirm). Moreover, it is also useful to know that the South Side Irish are, as they claimed, more communal than the rest of us. I must apologize to my classmates from the South Side, but for most of them that will have to wait until the world-to-come.

More to the point for the purposes of this book, as one might conclude from the interviews in appendix C, many of those who have drifted away from the Church seem to be immigrants and, indeed, to be Hispanic immigrants. Does the statistical data presented in the previous chapters provide any insight into the meaning of this phenomenon?

A brief summary of the findings so far seems appropriate. Religion continues to be community, stories (images, symbols, pictures), and leadership. The friendship groups and the parishes represent for Chicago Catholics the community dimensions of their religious life; the strong measures of religious identity (stories and rituals of resurrection, of the poor, of the Eucharist, and of the Mother of Jesus) create an attractive religious imagination that binds the community together, and the admired leadership presides over the community through administration of the Sacraments and through its preaching of the stories and the images. This unity, however, is not sustained by regular (i.e., weekly) Mass attendance and does not sustain acceptance of the Church's sexual ethic. Mass attendance is low because the laity find it boring, don't feel they get much out of it, and think the sermons are dull—this despite the fact that they give the clergy high marks on their preaching and other professional obligations. Nonetheless, their strongest criticism of priests and nuns is that there are not enough of them. The most recent cohort is especially dedicated but attracts little attention from the clergy and is described by some of the bishops as thoroughly secularized.

Appendix A

Survey Questionnaire

Changing Religious Attitudes

Hello, my name is _____

I'm… [a student at /calling from] the University of Chicago…

…conducting short telephone interviews as part of academic research…

…we're giving eligible participants $20 as a thank you for their time…

…not selling anything or asking for donations…

Describing the study:

The goal of the study is to learn more about people's opinions and beliefs about spirituality today.

The survey takes about 20 minutes or less. It consists of a few different kinds of public opinion questions about thoughts and beliefs on spirituality and religion. They are almost all multiple choice questions and [you/participants] can skip any questions [you/they] would rather not answer.

If asked how we got their number:

Your household was selected at random from lists of Chicago-area households, such as registered phone numbers and census information, as part of a small sample to represent the population as a whole.

First I need to ask you a few questions to see if you qualify for the study. May I continue?

QF-1: **IF Area Code is 312 or 773, SKIP TO QF-1.5.**

QF-1: **IF Area Code is 708, 224, or 847, ask: Which county do you live in?**
    ☐1   Cook [CONTINUE]
    ☐2   Lake [CONTINUE]
    ☐3   Other [THANKS AND TERMINATE]

QF-1.5: How many adults live in this household? _____
    [ONE, SKIP TO QF-1.7]
    [2+, GO TO QF-1.6]

QF-1.6: Of those adults, which one will have the next birthday?

Is that you or someone else?
    ☐$_1$ Person on Phone -> According to the scientific sampling of the household, you are the eligible respondent.
    ☐$_2$ Someone Else -> According to the scientific sampling of the household, that person is the eligible respondent

QF-1.7: What is (your/that person's) name? _____
‾‾‾
    [IF QF-1.6 IS "SOMEONE ELSE," GO TO QF-1.8]
    [ELSE, SKIP TO QF-2]

QF-1.8: May I speak to that person?
    ☐$_1$ Yes [SKIP QF-2]
    ☐$_2$ No [GO TO APPT]

APPT: [GET BEST DAY/TIME TO CALL TO REACH R, MAKE APPT ON ROC AND ON WHITEBOARD.]

QF-2: What is your current religious preference, Protestant, Catholic, Jewish, some other religion, or no religion at all?

☐1   Catholic → [CONTINUE WITH SURVEY, SKIP TO Q2 (P5)]
☐2   Protestant (any type) → [SKIP TO QF-3]
☐3   Jewish   → [SKIP TO QF-3]
☐4   Some Other   → [SKIP TO QF-3]
☐5   No Religion   → [SKIP TO QF-3]
☐-1   Refused → [SKIP TO QF-3]

QF-3: Have you ever been a member of the Catholic Church?

☐1   Yes → [GO TO AQ4]
☐2   2 No → [THANK AND TERMINATE:]

"I'm sorry; you do not qualify for the study. Thank you for your time."

[**IF ASKED:** "We're specifically looking for people who are or have previously been affiliated with the Catholic Church who are living in Cook and Lake Counties."]

[**IF ASKED:** "Why didn't you tell me that upfront?" Explain that some people might tell you they don't qualify when they do and therefore you cannot divulge the inclusion criteria up front. If they have any questions about this, they can contact **Colm O'Muircheartaigh.**]

IF QUALIFY:

MANDATORY IRB INFO BEFORE STARTING INTERVIEW

...the survey takes about 20 minutes to complete.
...participation is entirely voluntary
...you may refuse to answer any question or end the survey at any time
...everything you tell us is completely confidential and your name will never be associated with anything you tell us.

[IF R RESPONDED "CATHOLIC" TO QF-2, SKIP TO Q2 ON PAGE 5.]

[THE FOLLOWING QUESTIONS ARE ONLY ASKED OF RESPON-
DENTS WHO ANSWERED "1 YES" TO QF-3]

**How much of an influence were the following factors in your deci-
sion to leave the catholic Church?**

[THE "NONE" RESPONSE WILL INCLUDE ANSWERS SUCH AS
"IT HAD NO EFFECT" "I DO NOT AGREE WITH THAT STATE-
MENT" OR "I DON'T THINK THAT IS TRUE."]

[RANDOMIZE AQ4 TO AQ17]

		A lot	Some	Not much	None	Don't know
AQ4	The sex abuse scandal	$\square_1$	$\square_2$	$\square_3$	$\square_4$	$\square_{-2}$
AQ5	Insensitive priests	$\square_1$	$\square_2$	$\square_3$	$\square_4$	$\square_{-2}$
AQ6	Birth control teaching	$\square_1$	$\square_2$	$\square_3$	$\square_4$	$\square_{-2}$
AQ7	Too much change in the Church	$\square_1$	$\square_2$	$\square_3$	$\square_4$	$\square_{-2}$
AQ8	Abortion teaching	$\square 1$	$\square 2$	$\square 3$	$\square 4$	$\square_{-2}$
AQ9	Vatican Council	$\square 1$	$\square 2$	$\square 3$	$\square 4$	$\square_{-2}$
AQ10	Untrustworthy bishops	$\square 1$	$\square 2$	$\square 3$	$\square 4$	$\square_{-2}$
AQ11	Don't believe any more	$\square 1$	$\square 2$	$\square 3$	$\square 4$	$\square_{-2}$
AQ12	Too much politics	$\square 1$	$\square 2$	$\square 3$	$\square 4$	$\square_{-2}$
AQ13	Church obsessed with money	$\square 1$	$\square 2$	$\square 3$	$\square 4$	$\square_{-2}$
AQ14	One religion is as good as another	$\square 1$	$\square 2$	$\square 3$	$\square 4$	$\square_{-2}$
AQ15	Another church is more appealing to me	$\square 1$	$\square 2$	$\square 3$	$\square 4$	$\square_{-2}$
AQ16	Your spouse belongs to another church	$\square 1$	$\square 2$	$\square 3$	$\square 4$	$\square_{-2}$
AQ17	Role of women in the Church	$\square 1$	$\square 2$	$\square 3$	$\square 4$	$\square_{-2}$

QYEAR: When did you stop practicing Catholicism? [PROBE]

_____

_____

How often do you think about returning to the Catholic Church?
$\square 1$ Often → [SKIP TO Q92 (P8)]
$\square 2$ Sometimes → [SKIP TO Q92 (P8)]
$\square 3$ Rarely   → [SKIP TO Q92 (P8)]
$\square 4$ Never → Why?

_____

→ [SKIP TO Q92 (P9)]

[END OF FORMER CATHOLIC SECTION—SKIP TO Q92 (PAGE 9)]

First we have some questions we want to ask Catholics on their views about their Church?

Q2: How important is Catholicism to your life—extremely important, very important, not so important, or not important at all?
- ☐1   Extremely Important
- ☐2   Very Important
- ☐3   Not So Important
- ☐4   Not Important at All
- ☐-2   Undecided

Q3: How likely is it that you might leave the Catholic Church—very likely, somewhat likely, not too likely, not likely at all?
- ☐1   Very Likely → [CONTINUE WITH Q4-Q17]
- ☐2   Somewhat Likely → [CONTINUE WITH Q4-Q17]
- ☐3   Not Too Likely → [CONTINUE WITH Q4-Q17]
- ☐4   Not Likely at All → [SKIP TO Q18]
- ☐-2   Undecided → [CONTINUE WITH Q4-Q17]

If you should leave the Catholic Church whatever might the reasons be—which of the following might influence such a decision—a lot, some, not much, or none?

How much influence over decisions to leave the Church does . . . have?

[THE "NONE" RESPONSE WILL INCLUDE ANSWERS SUCH AS "IT HAD NO EFFECT" "I DO NOT AGREE WITH THAT STATEMENT" OR "I DON'T THINK THAT IS TRUE."]

[RANDOMIZE Q4 TO Q17]

		A lot	Some	Not much	None	Don't Know
Q4	The sex abuse scandal	☐1	☐2	☐3	☐4	☐-2
Q5	Insensitive priests	☐1	☐2	☐3	☐4	☐-2
Q6	Birth control teaching	☐1	☐2	☐3	☐4	☐-2
Q7	Too much change in the Church	☐1	☐2	☐3	☐4	☐-2
Q8	Abortion teaching	☐1	☐2	☐3	☐4	☐-2
Q9	Vatican Council	☐1	☐2	☐3	☐4	☐-2
Q10	Untrustworthy bishops	☐1	☐2	☐3	☐4	☐-2
Q11	Don't believe any more	☐1	☐2	☐3	☐4	☐-2
Q12	Too much politics	☐1	☐2	☐3	☐4	☐-2
Q13	Church obsessed with money	☐1	☐2	☐3	☐4	☐-2
Q14	One religion is as good as another	☐1	☐2	☐3	☐4	☐-2
Q15	Another church is more appealing to me	☐1	☐2	☐3	☐4	☐-2
Q16	Your spouse belongs to another church	☐1	☐2	☐3	☐4	☐-2
Q17	Role of women in the Church	☐1	☐2	☐3	☐4	☐-2

The following are some reasons people give for remaining Catholic. How strong a reason is each for you? Is it very strong, pretty strong, not too strong, or not strong at all?

How strong a reason is...?

[RANDOMIZE Q18 TO Q28]	Very Strong	Pretty Strong	Not Too Strong	Not Strong at All
Q18 You like being Catholic	$\square_1$	$\square_2$	$\square_3$	$\square_4$
Q19 You've always been a Catholic	$\square_1$	$\square_2$	$\square_3$	$\square_4$
Q20 You value the Mass and the Sacraments	$\square_1$	$\square_2$	$\square_3$	$\square_4$
Q21 It is important for you to be part of the Catholic community	$\square_1$	$\square_2$	$\square_3$	$\square_4$
Q22 You've known many good priests	$\square$1	$\square$2	$\square$3	$\square$4
Q23 Catholic ceremonies mean a lot to you	$\square$1	$\square$2	$\square$3	$\square$4
Q24 You're still attracted by Catholic feasts and celebrations	$\square$1	$\square$2	$\square$3	$\square$4
Q25 It is important to pass the tradition on to your children	$\square$1	$\square$2	$\square$3	$\square$4
Q26 There is something very special about being Catholic that you can't find in other religions	$\square$1	$\square$2	$\square$3	$\square$4
Q27 You can't imagine not being Catholic	$\square$1	$\square$2	$\square$3	$\square$4
Q28 Your spouse is involved and you go along	$\square$1	$\square$2	$\square$3	$\square$4

As I read the following, please tell me how important each aspect of Catholicism is to your Catholic identity? Is it very important, somewhat important, not too important, or not important at all.

How important is...?

[RANDOMIZE Q29 TO Q41]	Very Important	Somewhat Important	Not Too Important	Not Important at All
Q29 The presence of God in the Sacraments	$\square_1$	$\square_2$	$\square_3$	$\square_4$
Q30 The presence of Jesus in the Eucharist	$\square_1$	$\square_2$	$\square_3$	$\square_4$
Q31 Devotion to Mary the Mother of Jesus	$\square_1$	$\square_2$	$\square_3$	$\square_4$
Q32 Resurrection of Jesus	$\square_1$	$\square_2$	$\square_3$	$\square_4$
Q33 Concern for the poor	$\square$1	$\square$2	$\square$3	$\square$4
Q34 An Infallible Pope	$\square$1	$\square$2	$\square$3	$\square$4
Q35 A celibate priesthood	$\square$1	$\square$2	$\square$3	$\square$4
Q36 Rejection of abortion	$\square$1	$\square$2	$\square$3	$\square$4
Q37 Weekly Mass attendance	$\square$1	$\square$2	$\square$3	$\square$4
Q38 Confession	$\square$1	$\square$2	$\square$3	$\square$4
Q39 Daily Prayer	$\square$1	$\square$2	$\square$3	$\square$4
Q40 Angels and Saints	$\square$1	$\square$2	$\square$3	$\square$4
Q41 Emphasis on Social justice	$\square$1	$\square$2	$\square$3	$\square$4

Please tell me if you approve or disapprove of the way the following church leaders are doing their jobs.

Do you approve or disapprove of the job being done by...?

		Approve	Disapprove	Don't know
Q42	The Pastor of your parish	□₁	□₂	□-2
Q43	The Bishop, Cardinal Francis George	□₁	□₂	□-2
Q44	The Pope, Benedict XVI	□₁	□₂	□-2

On a scale of excellent, good, fair, or poor, how would you rate the priests in your parish on the following items?

[RANDOMIZE Q45 TO Q55]

		Excellent	Good	Fair	Poor	Don't Know
Q45	Preaching	□1	□2	□3	□4	□-2
Q46	Respect for women	□1	□2	□3	□4	□-2
Q47	Sympathetic counseling	□1	□2	□3	□4	□-2
Q48	Work with youth	□1	□2	□3	□4	□-2
Q49	Worship services	□1	□2	□3	□4	□-2
Q50	Personal warmth	□1	□2	□3	□4	□-2
Q51	Honesty	□1	□2	□3	□4	□-2
Q52	Kindness	□1	□2	□3	□4	□-2
Q53	Energy	□1	□2	□3	□4	□-2
Q54	Intelligence	□1	□2	□3	□4	□-2
Q55	Friendliness	□1	□2	□3	□4	□-2

[Q56 THROUGH Q68 ARE TWO-PART QUESTIONS. PLEASE ASK THE CORRESPONDING PART B QUESTION AFTER YOU ASK THE PART A QUESTION.]

How important is it to you that the Church responds to the following needs? For each, please tell me if it is very important, somewhat important, not too important, or not important at all.

How important is it that the Church responds to . . .?

[RANDOMIZE Q56 TO Q68, ASKING PART A AND PART B CONSEQUETIVELY FOR EACH ITEM]

		Very Important	Somewhat Important	Not Too Important	Not Important at All	Don't Know
Q56 A	Giving sense of the meaning and purpose of life	□₁	□₂	□₃	□₄	□-2
Q57 A	Providing a community to belong to.	□₁	□₂	□₃	□₄	□-2
Q58 A	Help in holding a marriage together	□₁	□₂	□₃	□₄	□-2
Q59 A	Help in the religious education of children	□₁	□₂	□₃	□₄	□-2
Q60 A	Help in dealing with elderly parents	□1	□2	□3	□4	□-2
Q61 A	Hope in times of trial and difficulty	□1	□2	□3	□4	□-2
Q62 A	Faith in a God who loves you	□1	□2	□3	□4	□-2
Q63 A	A heritage to pass on to children	□1	□2	□3	□4	□-2
Q64 A	Values to which to commit	□1	□2	□3	□4	□-2
Q65 A	Consolation at the time of death of loved ones	□1	□2	□3	□4	□-2
Q66 A	Preparation for your own death	□1	□2	□3	□4	□-2
Q67 A	An awareness of the spiritual dimension of life	□1	□2	□3	□4	□-2
Q68 A	More understanding of the mysteries of God	□1	□2	□3	□4	□-2

Looking at the same list of needs, in your experience how well has the Church responded to each? Would you say its response has been excellent, good, fair, or poor?

How has the Church's response been for...?

		Excellent	Good	Fair	Poor	Don't know
Q56 B	Giving sense of the meaning and purpose of life	□₁	□₂	□₃	□₄	□-2
Q57 B	Providing a community to belong to.	□₁	□₂	□₃	□₄	□-2
Q58 B	Help in holding a marriage together	□₁	□₂	□₃	□₄	□-2
Q59 B	Help in the religious education of children	□₁	□₂	□₃	□₄	□-2
Q60 B	Help in dealing with elderly parents	□1	□2	□3	□4	□-2
Q61 B	Hope in times of trial and difficulty	□1	□2	□3	□4	□-2
Q62 B	Faith in a God who loves you	□1	□2	□3	□4	□-2
Q63 B	A heritage to pass on to children	□1	□2	□3	□4	□-2
Q64 B	Values to which to commit	□1	□2	□3	□4	□-2
Q65 B	Consolation at the time of death of loved ones	□1	□2	□3	□4	□-2
Q66 B	Preparation for your own death	□1	□2	□3	□4	□-2
Q67 B	An awareness of the spiritual dimension of life	□1	□2	□3	□4	□-2
Q68 B	More understanding of the mysteries of God	□1	□2	□3	□4	□-2

Please tell me if you agree or disagree with the following assertions some people make about priests and nuns.

In general, do you agree or disagree that priests and nuns...?

[RANDOMIZE Q82 TO Q91]

		Agree	Disagree	Don't know
Q82	Don't understand what life is like for ordinary people	$\square_1$	$\square_2$	$\square_{-2}$
Q83	Are rigid about rules	$\square_1$	$\square_2$	$\square_{-2}$
Q84	Are autocratic	$\square_1$	$\square_2$	$\square_{-2}$
Q85	Think they have all the answers	$\square_1$	$\square_2$	$\square_{-2}$
Q86	Are not available when you need them	$\square_1$	$\square_2$	$\square_{-2}$
Q87	Are not fair	$\square_1$	$\square_2$	$\square_{-2}$
Q88	Don't have to earn a living	$\square_1$	$\square_2$	$\square_{-2}$
Q89	Don't seem to have professional standards	$\square_1$	$\square_2$	$\square_{-2}$
Q90	Won't share power with the parishioners	$\square_1$	$\square_2$	$\square_{-2}$
Q91	Are in too short supply	$\square_1$	$\square_2$	$\square_{-2}$

[**CONTINUATION POINT FOR SHORT VERSION OF SURVEY]**

Q92 Are you currently married, single, separated, divorced, or widowed?

- $\square$1   Married → [CONTINUE]
- $\square$2   Single → [SKIP TO Q97A]
- $\square$3   Separated → [SKIP TO Q97A]
- $\square$4   Divorced → [SKIP TO Q97A]
- $\square$5   Widowed → [SKIP TO Q97A]

Q93 Is this your first marriage?

- $\square$1   Yes
- $\square$2   No

Q94 What religion is your spouse? Protestant, Catholic, Jewish, some other religion, or no religion?

- $\square$1   Catholic
- $\square$2   Protestant (Any Type)
- $\square$3   Jewish
- $\square$4   Some Other
- $\square$5   No Religion
- $\square$-1   Refused

Q95   Were you married by a priest?

☐1   Yes   → [SKIP TO Q97A]
☐2   No   → [CONTINUE WITH Q96]
☐-1   Refused → [SKIP TO Q97A]

Q96   Please tell me why you weren't married by a priest
[OPEN ENDED; CODE FROM BELOW]

☐1   Previous marriage
☐2   Too many rules and regulations for Church marriages
☐3   Priest was hostile
☐4   We didn't want a Church marriage
☐5   Too expensive
☐6   Family Problems
☐7   Other

Q97a Do you have children?

☐1   Yes   → [CONTINUE WITH Q97B]
☐2   No   → [IF CURRENT CATHOLIC, skip to Q98]
              → [IF FORMER CATHOLIC, SKIP to QRACE (P14]
☐-1   Refused → [SKIP TO Q98]

Q97b How many? [ENTER NUMBER]

Number:_____

Q97c Do they currently, or did they once go to Catholic schools?

☐1   Yes
☐2   No
☐-1   Refused

Q97d In what religion are you raising your children? Protestant, Catholic, Jewish, some other religion, or no religion?

☐1   Protestant (any type)
☐2   Catholic
☐3   Jewish
☐4   Some Other, please specify: _____
☐5   No Religion
☐-1   Refused

→ [***IF R IS FORMER CATHOLIC, SKIP TO QRACE (P14)]

Q98   How often do you attend church services? Do you attend…?
[USE CATEGORIES AS PROBES]
☐1   Never   → [CONTINUE WITH Q100]
☐2   Less than once a year   → [CONTINUE WITH Q100]
☐3   About once a year   → [CONTINUE WITH Q100]
☐4   Several times a year   → [CONTINUE WITH Q100]
☐5   About every month   → [CONTINUE WITH Q100]
☐6   A couple of times every month→ [SKIP TO Q112]
☐7   Nearly every week   → [SKIP TO Q112]
☐8   More than once a week   → [SKIP TO Q112]

Please tell me how important a factor each of the following is as a reason why you don't attend church more often. Is each very important, somewhat important, not too important, or not important at all?

How important is…?

[RANDOMIZE Q100 TO Q111]		Very Important	Somewhat Important	Not Too Important	Not Important at All	Undecided
Q100	It's boring	☐$_1$	☐$_2$	☐$_3$	☐$_4$	☐$_{-2}$
Q101	You work on Sunday	☐$_1$	☐$_2$	☐$_3$	☐$_4$	☐$_{-2}$
Q102	It's not a mortal sin to miss mass	☐$_1$	☐$_2$	☐$_3$	☐$_4$	☐$_{-2}$
Q103	Sermons are poor	☐$_1$	☐$_2$	☐$_3$	☐$_4$	☐$_{-2}$
Q104	You don't get anything out of it	☐1	☐2	☐3	☐4	☐$_{-2}$
Q105	It takes too long	☐1	☐2	☐3	☐4	☐$_{-2}$
Q106	There are too many people running around	☐1	☐2	☐3	☐4	☐$_{-2}$
Q107	There's no sense of mystery	☐1	☐2	☐3	☐4	☐$_{-2}$
Q108	The singing is terrible	☐1	☐2	☐3	☐4	☐$_{-2}$
Q109	You can't pray there	☐1	☐2	☐3	☐4	☐$_{-2}$
Q110	There's too much noise	☐1	☐2	☐3	☐4	☐$_{-2}$
Q111	Too busy	☐1	☐2	☐3	☐4	☐$_{-2}$

Q112   How often do you pray?
☐1   Never
☐2   Rarely
☐3   Once a week
☐4   Several times a week
☐5   Every Day
☐6   Several times a day
☐-1   Refused

Please tell me if you think the following items are requirements to be a good Catholic.
To be a good Catholic, do you have to...?

[IF ASKED, WHAT DO YOU MEAN BY "A GOOD CATHOLIC,"
ANSWER, "IN YOUR OPINION, TO BE A GOOD CATHOLIC..."]
[IF R DOESN'T KNOW THE CHURCH'S TEACHING, CODE AS
"DON'T KNOW"]

[RANDOMIZE Q113 TO Q127]

		Yes	No	Undecided / Don't Know	Refused
Q113	Believe in the Resurrection of Jesus	□₁	□₂	□₋₂	□₋₁
Q114	Believe Jesus is present in the Eucharist	□₁	□₂	□₋₂	□₋₁
Q115	Donate time and money to help the poor	□₁	□₂	□₋₂	□₋₁
Q116	Accept the church's teaching that abortion is always wrong	□₁	□₂	□₋₂	□₋₁
Q117	Accept the church's teaching on the death penalty	□₁	□₂	□₋₂	□₋₁
Q118	Donate time and money to help your parish	□₁	□₂	□₋₂	□₋₁
Q119	Accept the church's teaching on divorce and remarriage	□₁	□₂	□₋₂	□₋₁
Q120	Have your marriage approved by the church	□₁	□₂	□₋₂	□₋₁
Q121	Obey the Church's teaching on birth control	□₁	□₂	□₋₂	□₋₁
Q122	Go to church every Sunday	□₁	□₂	□₋₂	□₋₁
Q123	Vote the way the bishops and the priests tell you to vote	□₁	□₂	□₋₂	□₋₁
Q124	Believe the Pope is infallible	□₁	□₂	□₋₂	□₋₁
Q125	Accept the Church's teaching on immigrants	□₁	□₂	□₋₂	□₋₁
Q126	Accept the Church's teaching on war and peace	□₁	□₂	□₋₂	□₋₁
Q127	Accept Church's teaching on gay marriage	□₁	□₂	□₋₂	□₋₁

Q128   Did you contribute money to your parish this past year?

☐1   Yes
☐2   No
☐-1   Refused

Q129 Did you contribute money to the Cardinal's Annual Appeal this year?

☐1   Yes
☐2   No
☐-1   Refused

Q133   Do you believe in life after death?

☐1   Yes, definitely
☐2   Yes, probably
☐3   No, probably not
☐4   No, certainly not
☐-2   Not Sure

Q134   Not including weekly mass, how often do you participate in parish activities?

☐1   Never
☐2   Once a year
☐3   Several times a year
☐4   Once a month
☐5   Several times a month
☐6   Weekly
☐7   More than weekly

Q 135   Would you please think about five people whom you consider very close friends, people you can really trust...

Have you thought them? I have two questions:

Q135 How many of them are Catholic?

☐1   None
☐2   One
☐3   Two
☐4   Three
☐5   Four
☐6   All of them

Q136 How many live in the same parish as you do or at least once lived in?

☐1   None
☐2   One
☐3   Two
☐4   Three
☐5   Four
☐6   All of them

We are now at the last section. I have some questions to help us to analyze the data.

QRace Do you consider yourself primarily White or Caucasian, Black or African American, American Indian, or Asian, or something else?

- ☐1   White or Caucasian
- ☐2   Black or African American
- ☐3   American Indian
- ☐4   Asian
- ☐5   Other , Please Specify _____

Q130 What ethnic or nationality group do you identify with? [CODE FROM LIST]

- ☐1   Irish
- ☐2   German
- ☐3   Italian
- ☐4   Polish
- ☐5   Other Eastern European
- ☐6   Hispanic
- ☐7   African American
- ☐8   English-Anglo
- ☐9   Other, Specify:_____
- ☐10   Mixed
- ☐-1   Refused

Q131 What is the highest grade of school or year of college you completed?

- ☐1   No formal education
- ☐2   Less than high school
- ☐3   High school graduate
- ☐4   Some college
- ☐5   2 year degree (AA)
- ☐6   College graduate
- ☐7   Some post college
- ☐8   Post college degree

Q132 How many years did you attend Catholic school? [ENTER NUMBER]
[ENTER '0' FOR "DIDN'T ATTEND", NOT '-4'.]

Number:

QAGE: Please tell me in which year you were born:

YEAR:

QSEX: [CODE WITHOUT ASKING IF YOU CAN. IF UNSURE, SAY:]
For the purposes of this study, I'm required to ask if you are male or female.

☐1   Male
☐2   Female

QBORN Were you born in Cook or Lake County, IL?

☐1   Cook County
☐2   Lake County
☐3   Other, Specify _____

Do you have any other questions or comments you would like to add?

_____

_____

_____

_____

_____

_____

_____

_____

_____

_____

Those are all the questions that we have for you now. We may conduct some follow-up interviews with survey participants to discuss the results of the survey when we have finished administering the phone survey. These follow-up interviews would be open-ended and more conversational than this survey has been. May we contact you again when the survey is complete to see if you would be interested in taking part in the follow up?

☐₁   Yes
☐₂   No

Thank you.

Now I just need to confirm your address so I can send you your check. I also just want to remind you that we retain this information separately from your survey answers and your name or any other identifying information will never be connected to your responses.

Name _____

Address _____

City _____Zip _____

Thank you very much for your time. I'd also like to tell you that the University of Chicago's Institutional Review Board (IRB) protects the rights of research participants. If you have any questions about your rights as a participant or feel your rights have been violated, you are encouraged to contact the Social and Behavioral Sciences IRB Office. You can reach them at [phone number]. I can also give you their address: 5835 S. Kimbark Avenue, Chicago Illinois 60637.

If you would like more information about the study and how the data will be used, please contact Colm O'Muircheartaigh, [phone number]. He is a professor in the Harris School of Public Policy and is the primary investigator on this study.

Sample Design of the Survey of Catholics: Sample Design, Response Rate, and Weights

Colm O'Muircheartaigh

This is a probability sample from all telephone households in Cook and Lake counties. The sampling frame for the survey was constructed from three separate components. From a commercial list vendor we obtained listings (with telephone numbers) of residents of Cook and Lake counties; these were identified as "Catholics" or "not Catholics," using commercial information in some unknown manner. Though our results do not depend on the assumption that this categorization is correct, we used the categorization to determine the optimum sampling rates in different parts of the population. We deemed it likely that the "Catholic" list would in fact contain a high concentration of Catholics, and that therefore the cost of calling and screening these numbers would be relatively low per respondent. The second part of the commercial list (designated as "non-Catholic" below) consisted of all other residents of Cook and Lake counties for whom telephone numbers were available; from this list we selected cases with a lower sampling fraction, as the expected cost per respondent could be expected to be higher as we anticipated a lower proportion of Catholics in this list. Finally, as residents whose telephone numbers appeared on the lists might be expected to differ substantially from residents whose numbers did not appear on the lists, we selected a further sample of numbers by randomly generating telephone numbers from all possible telephone numbers in Cook and Lake counties (designated as "RDD" below). As resolution and screening costs were expected to be much higher for this group (far more non-productive telephone calls), we selected from this frame with a much reduced sampling fraction.

This process of sample design produces interviews considerably more efficiently than sampling with equal probabilities from all potential telephone numbers in the two counties. However, if the Catholics in each of the three sub-frames differ from each other, it is necessary to introduce weights into the analysis in order to have the results reflect the true population structure rather than the configuration of the respondents in the sample.

Response Rates

CASRO[1] response rates: The overall response rate for the survey (shown in the column headed "CASRO" in the table below) was 40 percent. This is a very good response rate for a telephone survey by contemporary standards. High quality RDD surveys are generally between 30 percent and 40 percent; good opinion polls are probably in the low to mid-20 percents; and market research surveys are often around 10 percent (though recent reports suggest response rates as low as 5 percent for some market research/advertising surveys).

We present both a weighted and an unweighted response rate. The weighted rate is generally preferred as an indicator of the quality of the inference; the unweighted rate represents the raw percentage of eligible numbers called who responded, and is sensitive to the configuration of the sample. In the case of the Survey of Catholics, the response rates are quite close across categories, with sample members from the "Catholic" list being slightly less likely to participate. The overall response rate is 40 percent whether we use the weighted or unweighted rate.

Table AA.1

Overall, weighted

Resolution	Screener	Interview	CASRO
91%	73%	61%	40%

Overall, unweighted

Resolution	Screener	Interview	CASRO
90%	70%	63%	40%

By sample source

Sample source	WRN	Eligibility	Resolution	Screener	Interview	CASRO
RDD	28%	40.0%	91%	74%	59%	39%
Catholic list	81%	69.5%	90%	66%	63%	37%
Non-Catholic list	80%	38.9%	89%	74%	64%	42%

Description of Weights

There are three weights given in the data set. As a minimum you should use the baseweight (field *bswt*); this adjusts only for the differential probabilities of selection from the three parts of the frame. The weight you should use for most analyses is the one called *samp_weight*. This adjusts additionally for within-household selection; otherwise the estimates will be biased towards the views of Catholics in smaller households.

There are two weights you could use (*pop_weight* and *samp_weight*). Both weights take into account the various aspects of the design and implementation; the difference is that *samp_weight* is normalized (standardized) to add to 524 (the achieved sample size) across the sample [and SPSS deals incorrectly with weights unless you normalize]. If you want to get (not quite so reliable) estimates of the *numbers* of Catholics with particular characteristics, you can use *pop_weight*, but the standard errors SPSS will give you will be wrong.

Weights for the survey of Catholics were calculated as follows:

Base Weight

Base weights were determined by sample source as the inverse of the sampling probability; we fielded 1400 cases from each of three sources: RDD in 1+ banks in Cook and Lake Counties; a list of residential households in Cook and Lake Counties with telephone numbers flagged as being 'Catholic'; the remainder or 'non-Catholic' portion of the list. The baseweights for the RDD frame were adjusted to consider the possibility of overlapping with the two lists frames. Baseweights are as follows:

> if sample_source = "RDD" then
> $p1 = 1400/4535988.008$; *RDD;

> if sample_source = "catholic_list" then
> $p1 = 1400/205655$; *catholic list;

> if sample_source = "noncatholic_list" then
> $p1 = 1400/889045$; *noncatholic list;

The baseweights by sample source are summarized in the following table. These are essentially the inverses of the probabilities of selection in each part of the frame.

Table AA.2

Sample Source	Baseweight
RDD	3240
Catholic List	147
Non-Catholic List	635

There are three further steps in the weighting process:

The resolution rate is calculated for each frame: the percentage of issued telephone numbers whose status (non-working number, household, non-household) is determined.

The screener nonresponse rate: the percentage of working numbers for which the screener is completed.

The interview nonresponse rate: the percentage of eligible households contacted within which an interview is completed successfully.

Weights for the adults interviewed are obtained by multiplying the household weight by the number of adults per household.

Final Weights

Nonresponse-adjusted adult-level weights by sample source are as follows:

Table AA.3

Current label	Sample source	Cumulative Weight	Frequency
C	RDD	1036066	61
C	Catholic List	238136	268
C	Non-Catholic List	505911	177

The weights are then modified to sum to (a) the sample size— *samp_weight*, or (b) the population size—*pop_weight*.; this is an estimate of the number of Catholics in Cook and Lake County on the basis of our numbers. It corresponds to about 1,780,113 people, or 40 percent of the population of 4,433,914 adults in

Cook and Lake Counties. The eligibility rate (close to the expected 40 percent) suggests that Catholics did not systematically screen themselves out to avoid being interviewed.

Table AA.4

Variable	Sum	Sample Size (n)
samp_weight	524	524
pop_weight	1780113	524

Professor Colm O'Muircheartaigh is on the staff at the Harris School for Public Policy at University of Chicago and he is also the Sampling Director of National Opinion Research Center.

Note

1.   The Council of American Survey Research Organizations (CASRO) is an industry organization that sets standards for the calculation and presentation of response rates. The response rate for a telephone survey is based on three factors: the resolution rate, the screener rate, and the interview response rate.

Appendix B

Interviews in Depth

Some Preliminary Remarks

The first six documents I read were all from men and women who were from immigrant backgrounds. I had wondered after I had glanced through the preliminary interviews whether immigrants might have trouble adjusting to American parishes, particularly if the parishes which they left one way or another were of the same ethnic group or temporary ports in the storm in the region of the Archdiocese where they had lived. Yet who notices a nineteen-year-old Italian woman in an ordinary white parish and wonder if she has identity problems or an Indian woman who is well dressed. Or a couple of Italians in a non-Italian neighborhood and wonders whether they might be flirting with the Presbyterians. Or two shy young Latina kids who hustle out of church after Mass and avoid the local priest. And how many pastors have the time and attention to wonder about these young people who might be strangers At least four of the first had some warm feelings towards the church of their childhood and, as it turns out at the end of the interview were thinking about coming home. My Tucson pastor's "ACA"(alienated Catholics anonymous) approach may be the only way to approach such people. Among the first six, two mentioned fear of priests because of the publicity about sexual abuse. I give these people names which are not their own so they are more than just data. Parish priest that I am I cannot help worrying about them. Each of them had become a member of a "Conservative" Protestant Church. Each of them found Catholic devotion to Mary and the saints difficult to explain to their new Protestant confreres. The priests whom they may have consulted seemed to provide no effective argument against these objections.

Quantitative and Qualitative Research

Sociologists often compare Quantitative and Qualitative Research. The former seeks for numbers, the latter seeks for stories. The former searches for statistical precision and probability sampling. The latter for personal interviews which recreate the atmosphere and the emotions of respondents. The former can tell us that 25 percent of a sample has drifted away from the church and how they fit into the demographic and attitudinal distribution of those respondents. The latter wants to know how the lost sheep worked out their decision to leave and what happened later, whether they remained outside the sheepfold and whether and under what circumstances they might have drifted back. Both kinds of studies have their uses and their weaknesses. Both provide useful information and both leave some important questions unanswered.

Some sociologist (Wuthnow, Bellah) try to combine both. In this project the origins of the investigation were focused on sample survey research. However, the alert investigators at the Survey Lab advised that many of the respondents who are no longer Catholics seemed ready and eager to talk about their struggle with the Catholic Church and that it might be possible to add some "Qualitative" material to the report. The author is very grateful for their ingenious, sensitive, and persistent interviews which notably enhanced his understanding of Chicago Catholics.

Chicago Catholics: Qualitative Interviewing

June 13, 2008

Kate Flinner
Wendy Greyeyes
Joy Heafner
John McKellar

Final Report: Table of Contents

Abstract

This report outlines the results of the qualitative interviews conducted as a follow-up to the 2007 Survey of Chicagoland Catholics. These interviews took place as part of a practicum course on qualitative interviewing techniques. Five students registered for the course and conducted the majority of the interviews in conjunction with the course instructor, Kelly Daley, and teaching assistant, Vibhuti Ramachandran.

The class aimed to investigate the following research questions: why certain people leave the Catholic Church; if they may return and if so, what may induce them to return. We examined three categories of respondents pulled from the survey. We defined these categories according to the respondents' degree of affiliation, or lack thereof, with the Church.

More specifically, we intended to analyze the effect of immediate social networks and family conflict on people's decision to leave the Church. We found that among the respondents we interviewed neither factor plays a significant role in the respondents' decision. Rather, we found that the search for spirituality and personal crises played a stronger role in motivating this set of respondents to leave the Catholic Church. Among our practicing Catholic respondents, we learned that they find their Catholicism as inextricable from their own sense of personal identity, and despite some reservations about Church policy and recent events, most will not leave.

Section I: Who We Interviewed

In order to meet the timing and pedagogical goals of the class and still gather enough data, we decided to conduct approximately twenty-five interviews. We selected respondents from among those who completed the survey last year and agreed to participate in this qualitative follow-up. We identified three broad categories indicated in the survey from which to select interviewees:

1. Lapsed Catholics who will not return
2. Lapsed Catholics who may return
3. Practicing Catholics who may leave

We then chose three standard demographic variables to further sub-categorize the three groups: gender, age, and education. Accordingly, we drew up three quota cell tables to reflect each of the three categories of Catholics with as equal a distribution of the demographic variables within each category as the proportion of willing respondents allowed. These three tables appear below listing the respondent category type and their current disposition information.

Table AB.1
Target Respondents for Lapsed Catholics, Not Likely to Return.

Category	Disposition
Male 18-40 LT College	Completed
Male 41-60 College +	Previous Category-Male 41-60 College has been replaced with this category. 2 completes in this section
Male 60+ College+	Completed
Male 60+ College	None scheduled or completed
Female 18-40 College	Completed
Female 41-60 LT College	Completed
Female 41-60 College +	2 completed
Female 60 + College	Completed
Total	9 Completed

Table AB.2
Target Respondents for Lapsed Catholics, More Likely to Return

Category	Disposition
Male 60+ College	Previous R in category: Male 18-40 LT College, or Male 41-60 LT College. Could not reach either, and was able to get Male 60+ College completed.
Male 60+ LT College	Completed
Male 41-60 College +	Completed
Male 60+ College	Completed
Female 18-40 LT College	Completed
Female 18-40 College	Completed
Female 41-60 College	Completed
Total	7 Completes

Table AB.3
Target Respondents, Currently Practicing, Might Leave
In this category, females are overrepresented because we could not find enough males willing to participate.

Category	Disposition
Male 18-40 LT College	Scheduled
Male 41-60 LT College	Only one person in former category-(Male 18-40 College +.), unable to reach.
Male 41-60 LT College or Male 18-40 LT College	Only one person in former category (Male 41-60 College), unable to reach.
Male 60+ LT College	Completed
Female 18-40 LT College	Completed
Female 41-60 College	Completed
Female 60+ LT College	2 Completed
Female 41-60 College+	Completed
Total	6 Completed

Section II: The Interview Guide

Based on our review of the phone surveys and input from Father Greeley, we identified a number of issues that relate to the central research question. To address these questions, we developed a list of broad concepts to act as guides for the interviews:

- Family issues/Major life events as they impact R's decision to remain Catholic or leave the Church
- Social/friendship networks in and outside the Church
- Nostalgia for Catholicism
- Catholic vs. non-Catholic identity
- Views on the Church as an institution
- Attitudes toward priests

With each interview, we intended to not simply ask a series of questions, but to engage in a focused conversation with the respondent. We began the interviews with a broad question that sought to elicit life stories that are unique to each respondent. We used the following two opening questions most frequently:

1. What is your strongest memory of being Catholic?
2. How would you describe your involvement with Catholicism, and how has it changed over time?

From here, we delved into the themes that seemed most important to the respondent. With the two categories of lapsed Catholics, we sometimes began differently, for instance, by referring back to some of the questions in the original survey and the respondent's answers to them. A list of common probing questions, arranged by themes, follows below. Many of these categories overlap and some of the questions may fit under multiple headings.

Common Probing Questions

Family Issues/Major Life Events

- How were you and your family involved in the Catholic Church while you were growing up? (Or, what role did the Church play in your family life? If needed: how often did you attend mass? Did your family pray together, follow rituals/rules such as abstaining from eating meat on Fridays, during Lent, etc?)
- How has your relationship with Catholicism changed throughout your life?

Social Networks

- Are many of your friends and family Catholic?
- Who has been influential to your relationship with Catholicism, and how?

Nostalgia for Catholicism

- How much do you participate in Church festivities and ceremonies? And specifically, what kinds of traditions and ceremonies (e.g. Christmas and Easter)
- Is there anything you miss about being Catholic? (If lapsed)

Catholic vs. Non-Catholic Identity

- Do you consider yourself a spiritual or religious person?
- What motivates your church attendance and prayer habits?
- What makes someone Catholic?

Views on the Church as an Institution

- What about the Catholic Church would you like to see change or improve?
- What is appealing about joining another denomination or religion?
- Have some of the Church's teachings, for instance on divorce and remarriage, or abortion and birth control, impacted R's views and feelings about the church?
- Has negative publicity for the Church owing to corruption or the sex abuse scandal affected R's views and feelings about the church?

Attitudes towards Priests

- Do you personally know your priest or do you wish to know him?
- Do you consult with your priest about your feelings of leaving the Church?

Section III: Methodology

We conducted twenty-two interviews. The respondents are nearly equally distributed across categories and demographic groups (see tables above). Most of the interviews took place over the phone, often because many of the respondents who agreed to participate live in the far reaches of Lake County (Fox Lake, Waukegan, etc.), making the trip time and cost ineffective.

At least two interviewers were present at each interview: the primary interviewer and the note taker. Almost all of the interviews were recorded onto audiotape (some respondents refused to be recorded). Most interviews lasted around thirty to forty-five minutes, although some interviews lasted over an hour. Following each interview, the note-taker wrote up a detailed summary of the interview. Students and research assistants coded the notes using ATLAS TI qualitative analysis software.

Section IV: Common Themes

Although the following observations are not organized by respondent category, we find it useful to describe some of the most prominent themes that emerged from the interviews.

1. Role of Family in remaining or not remaining Catholic

It seems fairly clear that for many respondents, early experiences of attending Mass with their families are among their strongest memories of the church. Respondent 11019730 remembers how her father would take her and her sister to Church while they were young. More than one of our respondents attributed their Catholicism to a sense of obligation to the family or specific family members. For respondent 11030780, her mother wanted her children to get their confirmation as a "Catholic credential." Respondent 21027710 considers his church attendance as a "social thing, not a religious thing:" he accompanies his wife and her family to holiday masses—like Christmas and Easter. This respondent feels obligated to attend Mass at these times out of respect for his wife, rather than anything to do with the Church. Respondent 21026150 also has a family obligation—of a different sort—which keeps him going to church from time to time. He and his wife are raising their grandson Catholic to fulfill the wishes of his late mother, and that is why they take him to Church.

It seems that *transitions* within families (e.g., divorce, marriage to a non-Catholic, moving from one neighborhood another, etc.) also have considerable influence on the respondents' relationships to the Church. In particular, a few respondents noted the Church's negative response to divorce. For example, after divorcing, some women found themselves excluded from Communion and "cast out" by the Church. One mentioned that once she and her husband divorced, she began to drift away from religion in general, and sought support from the women's movement. Another added that the Church turned her away after she divorced her husband, and did not allow her to return until their rules on divorce softened a bit. She added, "I don't think God made that commandment, that if I divorce my husband for a good reason, that the Church should have recognized it and let me be" (31010830). Respondents were particularly hurt by the Church's rejection at a time when they "needed the Church more then than I ever had in my whole life" (31010830).

2. Major Life Events

Some respondents cited the death of a loved one, illness, or near-death experiences as pivotal moments in their religious lives. For example, one lapsed Catholic began to seek spiritual meaning after she was diagnosed with a serious illness. Eventually, she became a born-again Christian rather than return to the Catholic Church. Another said that when she was five her uncle was dying and was read his last rites. She went to the window to look up at God and pray for her uncle, and he remained alive for many years to come. It was at this point when she began to realize she wanted to be close to God (21008630). When she looks back at the moment, she said that was the first time she realized how important a personal relationship with God meant to her, and she was never able to "fill her spiritual hunger" as a Catholic.

In one instance, it was the death of a family member that changed the family's (and correspondingly, the individual's) relationship to Catholicism. Respondent 31006570 grew up in a fairly observant, traditional Catholic family, who attended Mass on Sundays and observed the sacraments. His father died when R was thirteen years old, which subsequently made his mother question religion and God altogether.

3. Religious Styles

Many respondents reported that they found other denominations' religious styles more appealing than Catholicism. One woman preferred the discussion and interpretation in her Presbyterian Church's sermons and Bible study groups; another preferred the enthusiasm she experienced in an Evangelical Church. A few respondents reported that the Catholicism they remember from their youth seems like empty routine, whereas their new religious practice seems more personal, meaningful, and fulfilling. Several of these respondents mentioned that personal relationships, socializing, and fellowship activities were central to drawing them to other denominations. Also, some of these same respondents indicated that they found Catholic priests either distant or unapproachable.

A related theme concerns what many respondents described as the "strictness" or rigidity of Catholicism. Respondent 11019730 described a lack of "freedom" in the Catholic Church, which she described as too rigid and regimented. She is uncomfortable with the "fear tactic" that the Church plays and the guilt it instills, as against the "freedom" she senses in her new Church.

At the same time, the unique pageantry of the Catholic Church seems to tie some respondents to the Church. For instance, respondent 21026150 repeatedly described Catholicism as "more religious" than other religions because of its specific traditions. Respondent 21027710 "does not possess the faith that religion requires," but continues to find the "spectacle" of the Catholic Church interesting. He enjoys attending holiday Mass because it is a "fancy thing." Due to his appreciation of these elaborate ceremonies, he prefers the Mass in Latin—it is more "fitting" with the ritual nature of the ceremony. He adds, "You shouldn't have to understand those words; you can't understand those words anyhow."

4. Closer, Direct Relationship to God

Among the respondents who have left the Catholic Church, all of those who are actively practicing Protestant religions mention a "closer relationship to God," when asked to explain what appeals to them about their new faiths. The fact that "you do not directly learn things from the Bible" in Catholicism was a concern for some, as was Catholicism's heavy focus on Mary. One woman mentioned, "Mary was wonderful, but she did not die for our salvation, Jesus did" (21008630).

5. Faith and Belief

For at least a couple of lapsed respondents, they left the Church because organized religion holds little to no appeal for them. They expressed the view that being a "good human being" is really all that is important. Two respondents discussed this at length, one of whom added: (she) "believes in a belief system, right and wrong and being a good citizen in humanity," but doesn't think she needs to go to Church on Sunday to put that into practice. And then there are lapsed Catholics, like 31006570, who feel no need for religion whatsoever. This respondent considers himself "too much of a skeptic" to believe in something that is not knowable or provable.

6. Attending Catholic School

At least three respondents talked about attending Catholic school as their earliest memories of the Church. For some of them, those seem to be the years in which they were most involved with Catholicism, and they gradually weaned away after their school years ended. Respondent 21027710 attended Catholic school for four years, during which time he attended masses regularly as his school program required. But he subsequently switched to a public school and stopped participating in the Church.

While Catholic school is among their strongest memories of the Church, these are often not good memories. Each of the three respondents who talked about their years in Catholic school had unpleasant stories to tell, such as being "bullied" (21027710) or "brainwashed" (31038430) by nuns. While respondent 21027710 said his experiences with the nuns did not affect his view of the Church as he didn't see them as "The Church," the other two respondents began to question certain aspects of what they were being taught during these years. 31038430 said she rebelled a great deal against many of the nuns' teachings, and 11030780 began to sense that "there was something a little silly about this organized religion stuff" when the nuns made her bobby pin a Kleenex to her head because women were supposed to have their heads covered in church.

7. Corruption/Scandals within the Church

Some respondents, when asked about frustrations with the Church, commonly cite money. They feel that the Church is far too obsessed with money, and this "greediness" runs contrary to the Church's emphasis on doing good. One respondent mentioned that the Church should use this money to help the poor, and not buy expensive robes and shoes (RB). Another mentioned that the money resulted in the Church being far too powerful (21014080). Several respondents expressed discomfort with the Church's finances, particularly among respondents currently considering leaving.

The priest sex abuse scandals had a great effect on how a number of respondents viewed the Catholic Church. As one put it: "if your neighbor molests a kid, he goes to jail, but if your priest does it" (21014080)? Respondents appear to be equally upset with the cover-up of the sex abuse as with the abuse itself. According to these respondents, the hypocrisy has shaken their faith in the institution, although they retain their faith and their Catholic identity. For example, one respondent told us: "Even a million dollars wouldn't make me step inside a Church," but she says the same prayers every morning that she has said since she was fourteen years old. She says she was baptized Catholic "and will be until the day I die—because of my beliefs." One person saw sexual abuse happen to his friends, which made him very wary of the Church. Others have sought religious/spiritual fulfillment in other Churches or practice their faith alone.

Section V: Analysis by Respondent Category

Category 1—Lapsed, Never Returning

Our analysis addresses reasons for leaving the Catholic Church for those lapsed Catholics who never intend to return. Motivations to leave fall into three main areas: emotional, spiritual, and intellectual motivations. Concurrently, we found political influences, such as issues of gender inequality or the sex abuse scandals, were not the primary motivations for leaving the Catholic Church.

Emotional & Spiritual Motivations. Respondents seeking emotional and spiritual guidance found other Christian faiths. These individuals expressed that the Catholic Church did not address their emotional needs or their desire to be closer to God. Respondents mentioned that other churches offered them guidance and a sense of comfort. These individuals sought out emotional fulfillment in addition to spiritual fulfillment. The latter speaks to broader concepts of God, creation, and existence; in contrast, these individuals sought out other churches to answer difficulties of their daily lives and their personal responses to these difficulties. The new churches more regularly and frequently helped them address quotidian feelings, actions, relationships and attitudes rather than larger questions of reality or God.

One respondent shared the following:

> ...and then I found this church, where the pastor is very dynamic and is into real life kind of thing. And even though I grew up in the Catholic Church, you never really read it the way—the way that he presented it, you know...and I think what drove me to this church is that he said there's no sense going to church if it doesn't help you live your life. (21040420)

Another respondent shared the church's guidance in negating thoughts of suicide:

> I remember feeling suicidal. And, uh, thinking, you better go get the pills before you do something strange. And then I'm sitting in church and the pastor preached on that very thing, on depression, and on how you can—send yourself there, you know. And, uh, what God says about that, you know, and he says, "you don't have to, I got your back, and your front and your side and whatever else you need. All you got to do is ask me. What do you need?" You know, and one of the things that he helped us—he helps us do is kind of always think about before you—you decide that all is lost, what is it that you need? (11030960)

Additionally, several interviewees explained their need to be closer to God. They felt the Catholic Church did not allow for a personal relationship with God, which they found in the practices of other churches.

One interviewee shared, "...everyday of your life you need God—gotta make the right decisions, sometimes when you're struggling in life you need somewhere to turn for answers. I feel Christianity provides those answers" (21014080).

These individuals continued to feel an affinity for Christianity as a whole; however, another Church better served their needs and offered them a means of expression with which they felt more comfort or personal affinity. Worship activities of their new churches offered greater opportunity to feel a deeper connection with God.

Intellectual Contradictions. Individuals who left the Catholic Church because of intellectual incongruities in Church doctrine moved away from religion altogether. They felt the creation stories did not resonate with their scientific understanding of the natural world. However, this disjunction was not limited to the Catholic Church but to religious institutions at large.

One respondent shared experiences with a sibling who recently began attending Church, not of a Catholic denomination:

> I grew up with him, he use to believe in evolution. Now he doesn't...you know people believe what they want to believe and that's okay, but you know, I personally don't think that God put the dinosaurs there to trick us. Or not trick us, I suppose, but to test us. (11030960)

These individuals question the premise of creationist stories and do not find any denomination of Christianity satisfactory in fulfilling their intellectual queries. Most identify as atheist or agnostic; they sample a range of spiritual practices outside of institutionalized religion.

Affiliation with Catholic Church. The "never returning" lapsed Catholic respondents continue limited affiliation with the Catholic Church. These ties stem mainly from family members or close friends who identify as Catholic. While most avoid attending even Christmas or Easter mass, some will attend baptisms, weddings, funerals, or other major Catholic events if invited by family. They do not feel nostalgia, or any strong affinity for the Catholic Church, however their love for family members and close friends keeps them affiliated with Catholic practices. Predominantly, Catholic social networks do not influence these respondents to themselves identify as Catholic. Instead, they serve to keep them in close proximity of Catholic people and practices. Concurrently, social networks have been significant for introducing lapsed Catholics to other churches. Most often, close friends have introduced questioning Catholics to new Churches. Social networks play a role in both keeping lapsed Catholics affiliated with the Catholic Church or seeking out new Churches. However, the decision to leave the church or institutionalized religious practice stems mainly from the individual, social networks serve only as mediators not motivators.

Category 2—Lapsed, Might Come Back

This category is composed of lapsed Catholics who indicated that they sometimes think of returning to the Catholic Church. We interviewed these people to see how and why some people think of returning after they have formally left the Church, as well as what might induce them to return.

For most of the respondents we interviewed in this category, their autobiographies indicate that they left the Catholic Church because it did not offer them what they felt they needed in a religious or Church experience. The majority searched other Christian Churches in order to fill these gaps. All but one person (who is uninvolved in any Church) in this category currently identifies with a Protestant Church denomination, most notably Baptist and Presbyterian congregations. Often these respondents offered rather specific explanations: "the Catholic Church did not have _____, but my new _____ Church has it." These missing things make Catholic liturgy and rules appear rote and empty, which subsequently makes mass dull or irrelevant for many of the respondents. More detail follows below.

Intellectual Reasons for Leaving the Church. Possibly returning respondents identified a number of elements missing from their Catholic Church experience and we organized these into three primary groups, in no particular order. The first is *intellectual*: some people showed that they desired more intellectual rigor and understanding of Christianity, which they could not gain in the Catholic Church. In the Catholic services, they saw the liturgy as incomprehensible or not open to understanding, and they also indicated that the Church offered few outlets for religious inquiry. They found these missing elements in Protestant Churches, which sponsor frequent bible study programs, have educational Sunday school classes, and in which the preachers discuss theological issues in sermons so that parishioners can understand Christianity better. One woman, who now attends a Presbyterian church with her husband and infant daughter, said: "I didn't find the Catholic Churches to be...very...informative ...there isn't really any type of preaching or teaching...I was just not getting anything out of Mass" (1103150).

She went on to discuss how she really enjoyed the Bible study sessions because they functioned as little theology classes. This echoes the feelings of several others in this group, who seem to prefer an active role in engaging in their religious experience.

Spiritual Reasons for Leaving the Church. The second idea some respondents found missing in the Catholic Church is a *spiritual* connection or experience in church practices. While no one doubts Catholicism's importance as a religion—one man even said, "the Catholic Church is more religious than the others"—some people seek a stronger role for that difficult to describe concept of spirituality, a transcendent religious experience. One woman found this spiritual feeling in her Baptist Church's emphasis on Jesus: "Well you see I was just not getting the spiritual food that I felt I needed from Catholicism." She repeated that it just wasn't what she needed. "In Catholicism they have a catechism and you don't learn from the Bible directly." Now she's in a Church that is Jesus focused, mostly evangelical—it's really rich in Jesus (21008630).

Social Reasons for Leaving the Church. A more involved *social* experience is the third element missing from the Catholic Church, according to some respondents. In a church setting, these people want to develop deep social relationships with other parishioners and with the clergy. They desire more than the obligatory Sunday morning greetings that they found typical to their Catholic experience. In the Protestant denominations, on the other hand, they enjoy the opportunities to build friendship. They find a great deal more camaraderie in the many fellowship activities these Churches offer. For example, these respondents participate in Sunday brunches after the worship service, Church retreats, and study groups. One woman, who now attends a Presbyterian Church with her husband and infant daughter, commented upon the sense of community she feels at this Church: "Yeah...I didn't get that in the Catholic Church, I never made any friends there, you know, I never really met the priest, I guess you could try to get more involved...but the Presbyterian Churches I've been to have definitely been more welcoming, more personal" (11013150).

These respondents' comments show that social interaction plays a significant role in their religious lives. They enjoy the deeper level of involvement that the sense of community provides them. Because this gives them a feeling of belonging, the socially involved environment seems to strengthen their emotional attachment to their newfound churches.

The Process of Leaving Catholicism. A number of the respondents spoke about the process that led them to leaving the Catholic Church and finding a new one. For many, it began with a friend or relative inviting them to attend a service at a Protestant Church. They enjoyed themselves, slowly began to increasingly involve themselves in various activities at the new Church—perhaps participating in a potluck dinner or a study group. This process continued until they eventually disassociated themselves with the Catholic parish they had attended and fully committed to the new Church. This *gradual* process points to two significant phenomena. First, it highlights the social appeal of the Protestant Churches described above. Secondly, and most importantly, it demonstrates that their break with Catholicism did not come out of a single, decisive event. Rather, their lapsing materialized out of a general dissatisfaction with their Church experiences.

Where They Stand Now. A single, traumatic memory or crisis did not cause the people in this group to leave the Catholic Church. Following from this, most individuals do not harbor overly negative and irreconcilable feelings towards Catholicism. Instead, they often looked back to the holiday services, Catholic school, or confirmation with a certain degree of nostalgia. We explored these sentiments for the possibility of returning to the Catholic Church. However, these people generally have only a fondness for their Catholic memories, but do not actively consider returning to the Church. It appears that their current contentment in Protestant Churches contributes to this circumstance. Said a female college student from Chicago, "You know, [the Catholic Church] will always be in my system, you know, and my mind...I just...I think the Baptist Church fits me more" (21000200).

Moreover, as a result of their continuing affection for their Catholic backgrounds, many of these individuals still participate in Catholic traditions for their families, but do not personally identify as Catholics any longer. A woman who now attends a Baptist Church affirmed that she has a great affection for the Catholic Church, because of her family life and her childhood. She still goes to Catholic ceremonies because of her family. She supposes that she keeps a combination of both the evangelical spirit that she feels today and her Catholic upbringing (21008630).

Therefore, Catholicism forms an important part of many of these individuals' identities in that it contributes to their personal history. Thus, they peripherally associate themselves with the Catholic Church through their family networks, but their current and primary religious identification belongs with their new Churches.

Category 3—Practicing, Thinking of Leaving

This section analyzes six respondents that identified themselves as practicing Catholics, but who "sometimes" or "often" think about leaving the Church. In this section, we distinguish between the respondents' actions and their thoughts. In the first case, we analyze the reasons that prevent the respondents' full departure from the Church. In the second, we highlight some major points that may trigger the respondents' thoughts of leaving the Church.

The first feature of our analysis is to determine what prevents those who consider leaving the Church from leaving. Respondents gave reasons of duty and devotion to the Church as the primary reasons for remaining Catholic. This sense is based on the embedded Catholic connection to their identity. These influences came early in their childhood from their childhood upbringing and family, ethnic, and cultural pressures. We also highlight one respondent's decision to stay Catholic because of his advanced age. Here we find it useful to discuss reasons for staying Catholic and reasons for thinking of leaving as separate dimensions. Although the respondents are not fully committed to leaving the Catholic Church, they appear to be on a trajectory to leave in the future.

The following quotations from the interview notes highlight many of the common reasons why some stay in the Catholic Church and the impetus for thinking of leaving.

Reasons to stay in the Catholic Church. A deep historical Catholic connection is a major explanation to stay in the Catholic Church for many respondents. The embedded history and experience of each individual's association to the Catholic Church can be categorized into several explanations: a matter of habit, cultural and ethnic connections, and old age as a major hurdle.

First, many consider the Catholic Church as being a significant constituent of their childhood upbringing. This embedded history with the

Church creates the feeling of familiarity and comfort that arise out of spiritual habit. Respondents feel a sense of duty and obligation when they think of themselves as members of the Catholic Church. This is not because of the pressures of family; rather this sense of duty is an internal self-awareness and personal identity.

> And then my friends in school, not as many were Catholic. They were varied, I had more Jewish friends, dabbling into eastern religion, or they were Presbyterians, Non-Catholics, so I was exposed to others. I still felt a part of me defend my faith so I wasn't really abandoning it. (21034050)

Respondent continues to attend Catholic church because she was brought up Catholic, she states, "Deep down it is instilled in me to go, and I still believe in the same way, even though there is a distrust of priests, I can't break away from the Church. The Lord is Lord and I can't break" (11033700).

Second, respondents felt peer pressure from their communities, and many view the Catholic Church as a significant part of their cultural and ethnic lives. Being a part of this ethnic and cultural group, there is an ingrained awareness that the Catholic Church plays a part in bridging that relationship to their ethnicity with no questions asked.

Respondent explains as a child, being raised in a Catholic Church, R didn't have a choice being involved with the Church. Respondent did her communion, baptism, and sacraments. Respondent states, "I come from a very Hispanic family and so the pressure to attend the Catholic Church has been pretty deep" (21025430). Respondent answers question about pressure from parents and explains, "Lots of pressure. You are Catholic or nothing else. There is no atheism, you can't be agnostic, you are Catholic (respondent speaks in a higher-pitched, authoritative voice imitating her parents). Everyone has been Catholic in Croatia since Jesus. So you just don't question it. And anytime I would ask for those answers, I would get the answer that it's the mystery of the faith. Which was basically I don't have the answers. That was just the mystery of the faith" (21034050).

Third, a respondent in the sixty-five and above age category explains that a switch to another religion at this point in his life is not "worth the effort." The respondent's self-awareness of age is the main determinant to stay in the Church making the respondent "too old to go."

> Well, I wouldn't really leave the Catholic Church now, because I'm too old now. All religions are the same, they all believe in being good to one another. I have my own interpretation of what the religion is and I'm comfortable about it. Because

of my age and because all my life I've been related to the Church, I don't think I would change my religion. It wouldn't be worth it, this is the Church I know and they are basically all the same in terms of religion. Differences among churches are based on the administrative part so I wouldn't gain anything from going to another Church." (11026450)

These respondents have considered leaving the Church, but continue to struggle with this decision. We found that the major influences affecting these respondents' justifications for "thinking of leaving" are the lack of spiritual connection and corruption in the Church. Below we further discuss the triggers that sparked the "thinking of leaving" attitude.

Triggers for Thinking of Leaving. Respondents explain triggers that sparked their desire to leave the Church. Two of the major explanations are the lack of spiritual connection and the perceived corruption occurring within the Church.

A lack of spiritual connection is identified as the most significant explanation for thinking of leaving. Some attribute this to all Churches being the same, Catholic homilies as too boring, or coming to the opinion that a connection to God does not have to come with the perception of being judged in the Catholic Church. In the following discussion, we define spirituality as a closeness and affinity to a higher being, and the Church as a means toward this higher power. Below, respondents explain the triggers that have sparked their interest in departing from the Church.

Respondent said the Catholic Church has been very "boring." "To me it's a loooong lecture. I prefer to attend the Baptist Church because there is more life to it" (21025430).

> By the time I was ready for confirmation, at the about the age of thirteen, fourteen, at that point, I was questioning my belief system in the Catholic Church. And saying I'm not sure confirming means you confirm your faith, and I don't think that's something for me, and my parents said "shut-up" that's what Catholics do. I was nine, ten, eleven....Every day in Catholic school, beginning at religious class everyone would give a prayer....These poor souls would be praying for souls not in heaven and hell. Then we get a message from the Catholic Church and they say, "Forget about that purgatory."

Purgatory resonated with R because to her it did not make sense. She said, "Now my prayers don't matter to me" (21034050).

> Well I didn't share with my family but over twenty years ago I had an abortion. You know it's not that I'm ashamed of that act but I know that they can't put any context to it. That was certainly a big life changing decision for me....even though I'm not a currently practicing Catholic, I did not denounce completely. I created an act that

is considered a sin in the Catholic Church, what does that mean?...It is between me and God and not between me and the Catholic Church. So that's how I separate that, and I still separate that to this day. Because I've recently went through a divorce. So I'm doubly damned in the Catholic Church, but that stuff is a little bit farther on. So that was probably a defining moment. (21034050)

R explains that [Protestant] pastors went up to the pulpit and talked and didn't talk about money, but focused on individuality, and that day in the world in everyday lives, to help people spiritually, and had respect, and didn't preach & holler—"they had respect for people" (11033700).

The second most prominent explanation is the perceived corruption occurring within the Church. Across all six respondents, this stood out as one of the most discussed topics. Many thought that the Church had to change church policy to address these issues.

Interviewer asks if R has ever thought about leaving the Catholic Church. She responds, "Yes I have...that there's too many things that have been going on in the Catholic Church, that violate...that I have not been happy with, about the priests and all that." JH asks her to explain, and R says, "the molestation going on in the Church with the priests and the children, and the fact that they hid that from the parishioners, spent a lot of the money to hide it and to free those men, those priests...the Church has turned away from its own people by doing that, they're preaching justice but justice was not done." JH asks about other factors, but R continues: "that happens in all Churches, but being the Catholic Church, being the biggest Church, there was too much hush-hush...those people came forward before and no one paid them any attention" (31010830).

Interviewer: Communion—
R: I will never take it, never. No way, with the priests who are out there today--no way. Never make judgments, God judges but you know what I have a brain, when I see people who have committed crimes and they become a pulpit person then it seems like it's always these people who have horrible lives, they are convicted felon, it's incredible." (11026450)

I follow the church's beliefs, but I don't believe in confession because you never know what the moral beliefs of a priest would be. I do my own thing; I pray on my own and think about God. I take the communion but I don't confess.

Interviewer: "Since when don't you trust priests?"

R: Since I was a child in Ecuador, I saw sexual abuse from priests towards my friends. It never happened to me but I know it happened to some other kids that I knew. That happened when I was about ten years old, before I did my first communion and then confirmation. So you never know what priests are like, even so Scandals happen in all religions. Not only the Catholic Church. (31018430)

These six respondents choose to stay Catholic because they feel Catholicism is ingrained in their identity. On the other hand, they consider leaving the Church because they do not feel Catholicism provides them with a spiritual connection to God. Furthermore, they are also bothered by the institutional problems within the Church, such as the sex abuse scandals and money issues.

Conclusion

In sum, we found that although recent events in the Catholic Church have upset many respondents, they typically do not constitute the primary motivation for leaving the Church. For those who have considered leaving, a strong personal identity or connection to the Church seems to override any feelings of anger or disappointment with recent events or even with the Church's stance on such issues as women in the clergy, birth control, and abortion.

Across all three categories of respondents, we found three similarities. First, all respondents—including currently practicing Catholics—share a longing for a closer spiritual connection to God than that afforded them through their Catholic practice. Secondly, within each group some respondents reported that a personal crisis (such as suicide attempt or a divorce) triggered their doubts about Catholicism or their need for a change. Finally, although we expected to find some relationship between childhood family conflict and current attachment toward Catholicism, this theme did not emerge among this set of respondents.

We were able to discern three important differences across categories of respondents. Currently practicing (but thinking about leaving—Category 3) appears to be more influenced by familial pressures to remain in the Church than respondents in other categories. They are also more connected to a sense of Catholic identity than the other two categories. Finally, although respondents in all three categories describe a search for spirituality, permanently lapsed respondents were more likely to discuss the ways in which their Protestant practice better met emotional needs.

Appendix C

Transcripts

1. Julio

Interviewer 2: Just to figure out what's going on in your own words. So, maybe to start, can you discuss how your involvement with the Catholic Church changed?

R: Oh, absolutely. Um, I was raised Catholic ever since way back when. And you know how, after you get to be a teenager and so I stopped going I think about fourteen or fifteen...

Interviewer 2: Okay.

R: ...was just the thing to do. And so I never really went back. And then I, I started having a lot of questions about the Catholic Church like it, like why can't priests get married.

Interviewer 1: Mhmm.

R: Why do we have to eat fish on Friday...why can't we eat fish on Friday? Um, I have a lot of questions. And they weren't answered. I didn't have anywhere to go. Why did we have to go to confession? I found myself making up sins just to go to the confessional because I had to go to confession.

Interviewer 1: And who did you ask?

R: I think family friends, people that I knew, um, you know, just, out of curiosity, the conversation.

Interviewer 2: Okay, you said it was the thing to do...

R: I'm sorry?

Interviewer 2: ...the time you left, fourteen or fifteen?

R: About fourteen or fifteen I think I stopped going to Church.

Interviewer 2: So, did you have friends who still went to Church and other friends who didn't go to Church or who weren't Catholic?

R: Well, you know what; this is really something because I grew up in an all-Jewish neighborhood.

Interviewer 1: Uh huh.

R: So, it was really kind of different. I was, my sister more so, was associated with the Catholic Church because she went to a Catholic high school. So I guess it was with my peers. So I really wasn't associated with the Church, and neither did my family go, so we just kind of drifted.

Interviewer 1: Where did you grow up, R?

R: In (*inaudible*)...

Interviewer 1: Okay, uh huh.

R: ...in [*city*]

Interviewer 2: Okay. So your parents didn't go to Church but your sister did?

R: Well, no. My father took us to Church every single Sunday until God only knows when...probably when we were about ten, and then we were pretty much on our own.

Interviewer 2: Okay.

R: My mother, I don't remember her going to Church.

Interviewer 2: Okay.

R: It was more or less my dad's responsibility.

Interviewer 1: And, um, if you don't mind, um, are you still ill, is there something...

R: No, I am. Um, we have a, I'm mercury poisoned.

Interviewer 1: Oh, okay.

R: From the fillings in the teeth.

Interviewer 1: Really?

R: Yeah.

Interviewer 1: How did you find out?

R: Well, after I was on my deathbed, one of the live-ins I had, I had a friend in the health care industry.

Interviewer 1: Mhmm.

R: And she told me about with diagnosis of having MS and silver fillings, and I thought that's ludicrous. I never heard of anything like that. Well, I started to read and I was crying, just crying. Every single symptom I had was mercury poisoning. And I found out from my hygienist, I had so much coming out of my fillings in the teeth, that I had them all removed. I'm still in a wheelchair, but I don't need to be MS anymore, the MS symptoms.

Interviewer 2: So, when did this happen?

R: This happened starting when I was twenty-seven.

Interviewer 2: Okay.

Interviewer 1: How old are you now?

R: I'm fifty-eight. I had to think about this for a second.

Interviewer 1: Um, and so when you say that you were on your death-bed, were your organs starting to fail, or you were in the hospital, or...

R: Oh, I was in the hospital bed at home. Last time I was in the hospital I was in for a month and a half, and they released me to come home because I couldn't take care of myself anymore, with a live-in.

Interviewer 2: So, after twenty-seven when you started searching for more meaning, how did you go about doing that? Did you, was it books, people?

R: Books, listening, um...oh, I know what happened. It started when, '82, 1982 in November. My sister said that she had an experience with the Lord. And I said you're nuts, get out of here, there's no such thing. And she said no, it's true. And so, I just kind of like put it on the back burner. And then there's a lady that was in management at the complex, and she took me over to [city]. And when we were riding in the car, she told me about her experience, and it was like one after the other. And I met this lady at the, uh, at the shore, and for some reason we started talking about the Bible, and she took me to Church, and I thought oh God, this is weird. Because you know the Catholic Church is so restricted. You know, sit, stand, do this, say this, whatnot, and was just different. And, um, then one of the gals that I used to work with at [*insurance company named*], which a born-again Christian, and she started telling me more about it. And I thought gosh, there has to be something to this. And I start reading, and reading, and reading, and reading the Bible. And another gal from [*company*] took me over, in [*city*], took me over to [*Church*], and that's when I accepted the Lord, and it has been wonderful. People think that, you know, you're nuts or whatever, but it's true, it happens.

Interviewer 2: It's not like a vision, you don't have to see something, just feel something?

R: Oh my gosh, yes. The next morning, I'm telling you, it was, um, I worked at corporate office over here in [*city*], and, uh, I walked in, and I loved everyone. It's like gosh, I'm loving people I didn't like. And it's like oh, it can't be, but it was. It was just the most wonderful experience.

Interviewer 2: An experience of love, maybe of connection, of oneness?

R: Yes, yeah.

Interviewer 2: Okay, and you felt that from your experiences?

R: Yeah.

Interviewer 2: At the [*Church*]?

R: Yes, in [*city*].

Interviewer 2: Have you been back to any Catholic services since?

R: No. Because, you know what, it's too, um, rigid. The Holy Spirit, you know, well I don't know what you guys are, but there's a Trinity, God the Father, God the Son, God the Holy Spirit. And it's a freedom. It's a freedom that I didn't feel in the Catholic Church. It was too regimented, you know, do this, do that, don't do this, do that. And it's a fear tactic. I felt a lot of fear.

Interviewer 1: So, if you didn't go to Church, you'd get in trouble or something like that?

R: Not trouble, but inside, you know, more a head thing, you feel convicted, you feel like you did something wrong.

Interviewer 1: Mhmm. How do you think that happens? Like, how does...how do you think...do you think that that happens to everybody who's Catholic, and if so, how do they do that?

R: Okay, how do they do that? Well, you know, take it like, um, no that wouldn't be the same thing...I was gonna say like the little kid growing up.

Interviewer 1: Mhmm.

R: You know, you can do this, you can't do that...

Interviewer 1: Mhmm.

R: ...you have to do this. Um, I would say in the confessional, you know, like the bigger sins, the more you had to do. It's just a thing. It's just, I don't know how to say it, but there is, there's a lot of fear, there's a lot of fear. There's a lot of fear that if you leave the Church what's going to happen. Um, how, I'm trying to think...it was like more or less like an unspoken word.

Interviewer 2: Is your relationship to your pastor at this new Church, is it different than your relationship to the priests before?

R: Well, when I was going, I'm not currently going, but when I was going before, it was like more or less you could go and talk to them if you wanted to. Um, it was pretty much open. And we could say and do whatever, you know, we weren't so rigid. It wasn't so rigid.

Interviewer 2: Okay, and then at the Catholic Church when you were young, were you able to talk to the priest then?

R: Gosh, I'm trying to think. Um, when I was young there was no reason to, so it, outside of just, you know, the hellos and you know, things like that. But we didn't go to Catholic school, we just went to Church on Sundays, and Catechism and communion.

R: Okay, in the Book of Acts, God is such a loving God, and there's such freedom. And people were healed, there was healing, there was, oh my gosh, there was, uh, there was preaching...I want to see the Holy Spirit lead the Church, and not fanaticism, and not some kind of quackery. But really to be able to lead the Church.

WOMAN: Mm-hmm. Have you had experiences with some kind of fanaticism?

L: Um, my friend has, (*inaudible*) but I never did.

WOMAN: Mm-hmm.

JM: Do you participate in any faith healing? Or just, praying about your health.

L: Oh my gosh yes. Oh I know I'm going to be okay. I know I am. But, I, you guys are probably thinking this woman is really weird, but it's true. You know what, if I can see it myself, I wouldn't believe it. But I saw that gal that was in my Church. She worked at [*hospital named*], she was a nurse and she injured her back, I guess from lifting the patients. And she had back surgery, and the doctor kind of slipped when he went in there doing the operation, and she became paralyzed. And she was also in a wheelchair. And her legs were so (*inaudible*) that they cut the nerves in her legs. And something like that, they weren't regenerated, and you wouldn't think that she could get up and walk, but she did.

WOMAN: Hmm. And where was this?

L: This was at Church, um, and it was in an evening service. And she sort of got up, and he said, "take your wheelchair and walk it outside." And she did.

JM: She had gone to their, was it a special ceremony or laying of hands?

L: No, no.

JM: Is there anything in particular you're looking for?

L: Yeah, the X-factor. Where there's excitement. Where there's people that really pray, that seek answers (*inaudible*).

JM: So you're looking for a certain feeling when you walk into the Church.

L: Yeah, you just know, and not anything fanatical, nothing control-ling, but just the freedom.

WOMAN: And have you ever experienced that yet, and you're just trying to find that again...

L: I did, we were going to a Church up in [*city*], and there was a starting of a move, and it was just wonderful. People were praying and they were seeing things happen. Like one service and the pastor was completely, we didn't know what would happen because the holy spirit just took over. Where there was people that were going up to the altar and just confessing their sins, and um, it was just remarkable. So yeah, there we started to experience that.

L: Yeah, they left. Um, it was, no, you know what it was, [*Church*]. Gosh I'll call you back with the name. You know what I could find out for you.

WOMAN: No, it's okay, I was just curious. Do you know why they left?

L: Yeah, because it was a disruption within the Church. Um, I think people were, you have to be so careful with control, because there are certain individuals with the Church environment that want to control, and it's not a good thing. Because when the Holy Spirit takes over, you give it to him and let him do it. Any kind of control, any kind of fanaticism is going to quench the spirit.

WOMAN: So there was some kind of disagreement or falling out of people within the Church or something?

L: Yeah, I would say so, yeah.

JM: Um, you mentioned that there were other parts of the Bible that were meaningful to you?

L: Oh my gosh, well, the whole Bible's important. It's like a road map to how to live your life. And God's still in control and he's going to do whatever he wants to. Um, well I like reading the New Testament, but I also like reading the Old Testament. Because I like, you know that promise, like Abraham. Abraham was promised that he would have his son Isaac. Well, back then he didn't know that it would be Isaac, but, he uh, God had given him that word. Twenty-five Years later, Isaac had come into being. So that's exciting to me.

WOMAN: Mm-hmm. Do you have children yourself?

L: No, I don't.

WOMAN: Okay. Are there any other parts of the Bible that you're interested in?

L: Oh gosh, the whole thing. Joseph, the Red Sea. And you know what, it's really funny, but um, the experience, with the Red Sea, you read it, you know that story right?

WOMAN: Okay. Now, do you ever think about going back to the Catholic Church?

L: No.

WOMAN: Do you have any friends that are Catholic?

L: Yeah, I do, believe it or not.

WOMAN: And um, do you talk to them at all about your faith, or their faith?

L: Yeah, they're born again believers also, but they choose to go back to the Catholic Church. You know whatever they want to do that's fine.

JM: Do they just go to Mass, or are there other special meetings or practices that might be closer to them?

L: Well, one of ladies is closer to her eighties, so I don't think she will go into, any kind of programs or anything like that. The other one, she works for the rectory, and she goes to a Catholic Church, but I don't know the answer to that question.

WOMAN: And um, do you have any strong memories? Can you tell me what your strongest memory of being raised Catholic is?

L: Let's see...gosh...I don't know if it was positive.

WOMAN: That's okay, it can be positive, or negative, whatever comes to mind as your strongest memory.

L: The Novena. I remember we used to go on Thursday evenings, and my mom and her friend used to go also, and we used to say Novena for, (*inaudible*) special requests. That's about the strongest thing I can remember.

WOMAN: Um, so but earlier, you said your mom didn't go to Sunday Mass?

L: No, she didn't. I don't ever remember her going.

WOMAN: But she did go say Novena's on Thursday evenings?

L: Yeah, of course, you know, she would go if there was a wedding, or if there was some kind of a function, but other than that I don't remember, I don't remember her going.

WOMAN: Okay.

JM: So you would identify yourself as a Christian correct?

WOMAN: Yes, born again Christian.

JM: For you, what's the most important part of that identity?

L: I'm sorry the most important what?

JM: What's the central, thing to that?

L: Um, it's having a relationship with God. It's just like, um, wonderful, remember the beginning of Genesis, with Adam and Eve, and how they walked in the garden? And they were constantly talking, believe it or not. And that's how it is. It's like a relationship.

JM: A relationship with God?

WOMAN: And how is that different from being a Catholic?

L: Because being a Catholic, there was no relationship. There was no hard knowledge. It's was just different. Are you guys both Catholic?

WOMAN: Um, no, were both just students, I mean, I teach a class, the point of this is not, were not coming from a religious perspective, we're coming from a sociological perspective, um, we're trying to understand, you know, we conducted a survey that asked some questions, that we called close-coded questions, you know, like multiple choice questions, and when you ask those of a lot of people, you can see big trends and patterns across different groups of people and the distribution of those opinions, but you don't get the stories behind them. It's two different kinds of methodologies, but if you talk to someone like the way we're doing now, it's open ended, we're hearing your story, you might have answered a question on the survey that asked "have you been Catholic" and you said, "yes," and then we asked you another question, "would you ever return to the Catholic Church," and you said "no," um, we don't get the whys behind that. We asked some other things too, like "are the following things reasons why you left the Catholic Church" and there might be, but there might be some other things. When we're talking to you in this sort of way, we get richer set of data that help us understand better.

L: You know, I think, in my personal opinion, if the Catholic Church would center on God, not just in theory, and not just say so, but really center on who God is, and the relationship with him, and tell their parishioners, about their, yeah, there is a relationship. And you know what? They baptize babies when they're born? That doesn't make a difference, well, if the babies dies anyway, if their, because they're not of an age of accountability, they're going to go to heaven anyway. But you have, you have to make a conscious choice about whether you want to accept Jesus Christ as your savior. I was never told that as a Catholic, I was just told, yeah, we have Christ, therefore, I'm a Catholic, but that's not it, there's more to it.

WOMAN: Can you say what that is? What there is that's more?

L: The more to it, is that the person needs to make a conscious choice to accept Christ as their savior. When I was going to Catholic Church, they never brought that up, never said anything, and I was always under the assumption that, yeah, I know the Lord does it, and they don't, they really don't, and that's what I think the Catholic Church needs to do. They need to tell people about accepting Jesus Christ as their savior, it's a heartfelt thing, and they need to confess it before the Church, and it's something you have to do internally. But the Catholic Church never did that.

JM: Um, we talked about confession and salvation. Do they feel different in born again Christianity than they did in Catholicism?

L: Oh my gosh yes. Because you know what, you know if you do something wrong, you know if you're not right, and you go directly to God, and you repent of it. And you're okay. Because you know what, that's why he died for us. He took away all the sins; he took away all your sins, as far as east is from the west. He doesn't remember them anymore.

WOMAN: Is there anything else you would like to add, maybe how your life has changed or how your relationship with Catholicism has changed over the years?

L: How it's changed with Catholicism?

WOMAN: Well, how your religious life has changed over the years, let's put it that way.

L: Yeah, just accepting Christ as my savior, and knowing that I know that's there's life eternal, and knowing where I'm going to go when I die, and that's gonna be forever and ever. And that's uh, a delusion that the Catholic people are under. If they're just going into a roped kind of mentality.

L: You know, I live in an area where there are a lot of Polish people. And they're very Catholic, well they're Catholic oriented, and they're very very much into Mary, more so than Jesus, and it's like, why?

WOMAN: Do you have any guesses, or any hypotheses…

L: I think that in the Catholic Church, maybe that's what they were taught.

WOMAN: And do you have any guesses as to why the Catholic Church finds her so important?

L: I don't, I really don't. I mean, besides being the mother. I mean, grace is the one that did the miracles. He was the one that taught the gospels, and so…

***

Julio is a classic case of the Catholic immigrant caught up in the "social disorganization" phase of the acculturation process into American society. He could appear as a character in *The Polish Peasant in Europe and America*. His parents do not attempt to support any religious path for him. He doesn't live in a Catholic neighborhood. The instruction he receives in Catholicism is weak. He seems to have had little contact with his parish, which probably does not attempt to sustain the Latino culture that was his heritage. Catholicism means little to him because it does little to support him while he attempts to adjust to American life. His background is probably Puerto Rican rather than Mexican (which would have no trouble with Guadalupe). He finds religious answers in a combination of evangelical services and spiritualist interests inherited from his mother. He fends off Catholicism with the biblical ideology of fundamentalism. Catholicism has let him down, though there probably has not been enough contact with Catholicism for him to see it as part of his heritage and a possible religious answer.

2. Jenny

Interviewer: So, we noticed from the survey that you mentioned, um, that your family had left Catholicism, um, when you were 8?

R: Yeah, about that time.

Interviewer: Around that time? Um, I mean, can you explain a little bit more about that time in your life, like what were the reasons?

R: Um…

Interviewer: Like…

R: Well, there…there were a lot of reasons. Um, I'm…I'm guessing I based the eight years old on, um, that was when I made my first communion.

Interviewer: Oh, okay.

R: And, um, you know, you have to go through all those CCD classes and all of that stuff before you get to do that. Um, and the only thing I learned in class was how to play a killer game of, uh, hangman.

Interviewer: Okay.

R: So, um, it just…I think my parents really just fell out of believing what the Church believed in.

Interviewer: Mmm hmm.

R: Um… my dad not as much as my mother. He kind of fell out of it longer. But we…we really kind of stopped going to Church around that time, um, regularly. Um, we would go…we continued going for midnight mass and for, um, thing…or, uh, for Christmas and for the Easter holiday we would go. And that was really it. We were, you know, holiday Catholics, I guess you would call it.

Interviewer: Mmm hmm.

R: And then we really kind of stopped doing that, too, because of, um, you know, there was so much upheaval going on in the Church and you're hearing all these different scandals and they were always asking for money.

Interviewer: Mmm hmm.

R: And we just didn't see…it wasn't doing anything for us. And my mom really doesn't believe in the Church, um, to say right… right out there. She…she's way out there in left field with her beliefs now. So, um, you know, she believes in UFOs and…(LAUGHTER)…all of that stuff. And…or at least would like to believe that she believes, you know. And…and it's not that she disbelieves in God or anything like that, but she…you know, she really reads a lot of those, you know, out there science books and Freudian Times and all of those different sorts of things and Fate Magazine and is very interested in the paranormal, and just didn't think the Church was open minded enough to explore other options, I guess you could say.

Interviewer: Mmm hmm.

R: So that was kind of what was going on.

Interviewer: Yeah?

R: Yeah.

Interviewer: And, um, in terms…because you mentioned you were holiday Catholics for a while?

R: Yeah.

Interviewer: So how long was that time period?

R: The last time I remember going to midnight mass was my senior year of high school.

Interviewer: Yes.

R: Now, my brother got married young. Um, he was 19 and his wife was very into her Baptist Church. And we have gone to, um, Christmas… I guess it's a mass…at her Baptist Church a few times with them.

Interviewer: Okay

R: But maybe…and really it was more of a something to do with the whole family and a whole lot less to do with the religious aspect of it.

Interviewer: Right.. Yeah. Uh huh.

R: So, you know, maybe three or four times since they've been married and they've been married ten years now. So…

Interviewer: And you mentioned your dad was less, um…

R: Well, he…it's…it took him a lot longer to…to kind of really fall away from his… his beliefs in…in the Church. Um, he went to Catholic school, he went to Catholic high school.

Interviewer: Mmm hmm.

R: Um, you know, had Jesuit priests that were his…his teachers all the way through high school, you know. So, um, I think he was a little bit more grounded…

Interviewer: Mmm hmm.

R: ...in the religion than my mother was because she went to...to, uh, public school all her life. So, you know, it was a little bit more pounded into him. But over the years, also, with him and seeing the scandals and what's been going on in the Church and, um, I don't want to blame science, but you know, learning more about the world, learning more about science and...and having his mind opened, you know. He believes in evolution and, you know, a lot of things that are no-no's in parochial schools.

Interviewer: Right.

R: And so, you know, when he started really looking at, you know, well, if they're no-no-ing this and it's so blatantly obvious to me, um, you know, well, what else are...are they, you know, telling me that I don't believe in? So, you know, I would say he was about, mmm, five to eight years behind my mother in his...

Interviewer: (*laughter*)

R: ...you know, falling out of...of, uh, his beliefs along the way. So...

Interviewer: And how would you say you, uh, fit into this?

R: Um...I am a non-Church-goer. I can't...you know, I don't go to Church regularly for anything. I...I admit I did get married in a Church, in a Lutheran Church, but I did that more for, um, the sake of the rest of the family...

Interviewer: Okay.

R: ...I guess you could say. And I had a really good friend who was a...happened to be a Lutheran minister.

Interviewer: Oh. (*laughter*)

R: So, you know, I mean, it all sounds kind of, you know, odd, but um, I would say that I'm very open to other ideas in other religions.

Interviewer: Yes?

R: Um, I'd like to think that I'm spiritual, but I'm not religious. Does that make sense?

Interviewer: Yeah, yeah. Yeah. Could you talk a bit more about that? That's very interesting.

R: Um, well, like I said, my mother really got into like, you know, all the weird esoteric stuff, you know, everybody...

Interviewer: (*laughter*)

R: So, you know, I mean, we really kind of... you know, we...we would spend summers, you know, in the library and, you know, one summer we studied...and not that we were studying in particular, but we just got interested in. And I have a sister who's almost nine years older than I am...

Interviewer: Mmm hmm.

R: ...and then, you know, my mom. I have a brother also. He's two years older than me. And, you know, one summer we got really interested in witchcraft and the paranormal and we read everything we can read about that in that it...you know, we're, you know, reading all about the Wiccans and...and the nature religions.

Interviewer: Right, right.

R: And then we read everything we could find about UFOs and then everything we could find about, you know, various other religions. And I kind of stuck with that. I took, um...

Interviewer: Yeah?

R: I think the most important class I took in my college years was anthropology classes.

Interviewer: Oh, yeah.

R: And, um, I think everybody should have to take all the anthropology classes there are.

Interviewer: That's good to know. I'm an anthropologist.

R: Yeah. (*laughter*)

Interviewer: Yeah.

R: So I started at [*community college*] with [*name of teacher*].

Interviewer: Mmm hmm.

R: And, um, he was just an excellent teacher and learning about, you know, not just the...you know, the different types of bones in evolution and stuff, but really talking about different peoples and their cultures and what they believe in and, you know, why they might believe in this sort of spirituality or why they might not believe in anything at all. And it...it was just really kind of interesting. Um, and I think it really added to, uh, I can't really say my belief system because I'm not really sure what my belief system is yet, but that, um, you know, there's something out there because there wasn't a culture out there that we found that didn't believe in something, you know. And there were so many similarities in belief systems, um, even where there were, you know, great differences in other ways, but through, you know, there's always these, you know, links that you can follow.

Interviewer: Um, and so are these times, um, you don't ever...do you feel, uh, like ever going back to the Catholic Church, sort of being there and, you know, maybe the music or the prayers or something?

R: Well...

Interviewer: Or is that something you really have left behind and, you know, aren't gonna go back?

R: It's...the pomp and circumstance is kind of fun sometimes. I always enjoy a good Catholic wedding, if you've got a good priest who doesn't put you to sleep.

Interviewer: Uh huh.

R: I...and my cousin had a great priest and...and he's just a riot. And...and he's...he's a lot of fun. And not that Church needs to be about fun, but he's not overbearing and constantly telling everybody that they're going to Hell.

Interviewer: Mmm hmm.

R: And, um, I appreciate that because I don't believe everybody knows that all the time.

Interviewer: Right.

R: And, um...but now I can't see myself going back regularly.

Interviewer: Mmm hmm.

R: You know, I go for weddings, I go for funerals. Um, if I were to be invited by, you know, another family or friends, you know, to do a holiday or some such, I would certainly consider it. Um, but I wouldn't go there looking for God, I don't think.

Interviewer: Okay.

R: If that's what you're looking for, I don't think...I don't think you need to be in a Church to find God. I think it helps some people focus on what they're trying to achieve or find their peace of mind or get that sense of community that people are often looking for in a Church. And I understand why people need that and want that, that makes sense to me. But I just think that a lot of our organized religion systems have gotten very corrupted. So...

Interviewer: Um, if you had to explain it, like would you say that it's...is it...it's the...so you're not, say, praying. If it's not in sort of an organization, constructive form, would you say it's more like a personal dialogue or a sense of connection with something else or...

R: Um...

Interviewer: ...how would you say...

R: Yeah, I guess it would be kind of a personal dialogue. Um, it...meditating, sort of.

Interviewer: Uh huh.

R: Um, sort of a way to just focus sort of...you know, like right now I'm going through, um...uh, fertility issues. So we've been going through

IVF, in vitro, several, several tries. And you know, that's a...it's a really crazy, heartbreaking thing to go through.

Interviewer: Mmm hmm.

R: And, you know, you do find yourself sitting at times thinking, you know...whether you think, oh God...and, you know, I do, because you grow up thinking in those terms. Oh, God, please let this work, please let me be healthy, please let me, you know, get through this or...and have the baby. And, you know, um, but do I necessarily really think I'm talking to God?

Interviewer: Yeah?

R: I'm not so sure, you know?

Interviewer: (*laughter*)

R: You know, you say these things and...and it's conditioning, I believe. I mean, you know...

Interviewer: Yeah.

R: I think anybody except for somebody who's truly an atheist, I think has those moments where they think, oh God, and they really mean, oh, let there be some God or force in the universe or...

Interviewer: I see.

R: You know.

Interviewer: Right. Well, I'm glad you can look at that so objectively, like...

R: (*laughter*)

Interviewer: ...extract yourself from the situation and think about, oh, that's what I'm actually thinking. That's...

R: Yeah. And I'm telling you, it was the anthropology class. (*laughter*)

Interviewer: Oh, yes, for sure.

R: You know, it's all about, okay, well, let's look at this from this point of view.

R: You know, if I were studying this, what would I be thinking? So...

Interviewer: Yeah so that's...that's very cool. Unh, when you said that, you know, some organized religions, um, can be corrupted these days...

R: Yeah.

Interviewer: ...do you...were you talking about misusing money or other things?

R: Oh, all sorts of things. I think there's abuse of money. I think there's abuse of power.

Interviewer: Mmm hmm.

R: I think there's abuse of people. Uh, physically, mentally, you know, various different ways. I think that many of our organized religions are very patriarchal.

Interviewer: Right.

R: And set up as such for power reasons. You and I just don't think that if there is a God, that that's the way God would want it to be.

Interviewer: (*laughter*) Mmm hmm.

R: I just find a hard time believing that. You know, um, I understand Churches asking for donations of money because they are in theory not-for-profit organizations. But, you know, the Catholic Church is the richest, wealthiest organization on the planet.

Interviewer: Uh huh. Right.

Interviewer: That was…you know, what if they had not been that way and if they had sort of been more, uh, orthodox Catholics and, you know, hadn't questioned the Church themselves? Would you have…

R: Um, you know, it's hard to say because, you know, I think that your upbringing molds you a lot. I would like to think that, you know, I would have continued to form my own opinions and still become the same person that I am, but I don't know that that's true because I think that…I think you are really molded by the way you're raised.

Interviewer: Mmm hmm.

R: Now, my cousin, who I'm very close with and we were very close with the family growing up. It was actually my father's cousin, so uh, their kids, uh, and me, we're of the same age.

Interviewer: Yeah.

R: Uh, they went to Catholic grade school, Catholic middle school, Catholic high school and then, uh, she went off to college. Um, she has fallen out with the Church, but much less so than me.

Interviewer: Uh huh.

R: I would say she doesn't go to Church regularly. Um, but I think she still believes more than I do, I guess you could say. I mean, she doesn't necessarily believe that she needs to go to Church every day and…or every weekend or, you know…

Interviewer: Right.

R: …that sort of thing. They do go for the holidays. Um, but I think they even go for the holidays more to make the grandparents happy than really anything else.

Interviewer: Mmm hmm.

R: You know, but I think she still believes in God and Jesus Christ and the whole kit and caboodle more than I do.

Interviewer: Right.

R: I mean, I know she believes in evolution and that, you know, the Genesis story is a… is a story, it's a teaching story, and things like that. But I think she still has a lot more Catholic in her than I do.

Interviewer: Mmm hmm.

R: You know, I have a tendency to look at the Bible as teaching stories and ways to set up rules and laws and whatnot and…and she still looks at it a little bit more as, even though it was written by men, that, you know, it's still a little bit more the word of God, you know.

Interviewer: Uh huh.

R: So, you know, I don't know. But, like I said, she was raised in it completely, you know, from start to finish, I guess you could say. So I guess there's my comparison, you know. So I don't know, I think maybe if my parents had been, you know, really, really Catholic that maybe I would have been more. But I…I don't think…I have to say, I still don't think I'd be going to Church every Sunday. You know, just because I just don't…I don't like where they've gone with the Church. I don't like the…the scandals that you hear about. I don't like the politics of it.

Interviewer: Mmm hmm.

R: So, you know, I like to think that I would be my own person.

Interviewer: Right, right. What about, uh, what about your siblings? You mentioned your brother and your sister. Um, are they part of it?

R: My sister is…she completely thinks of the Church as crap.

Interviewer: (*laughter*)

R: I can tell you, those are her exact words because we had this conversation a couple weekends ago.

Interviewer: Oh, I see.

R: They had a Mother's Day, uh, breakfast thing and my mother, my grandmother and my sister all wear pants because they're not skirt-wearing girls.

Interviewer: Right. (*laughter*)

R: And the dirty looks…

Interviewer: Oh, boy.

R: …that, you know, they got for wearing pants in the Church, you know, and…and Kim heard about it later, you know.

Interviewer: Oh, wow.

R: And they told her, you know, you should have told your parent…your…your…your mother-in-law that, you know, that was not a way properly to dress in Church. And then, uh, you know, so that kind of stirred up my whole, okay, I've had enough of this place.

Interviewer: (*laughter*)

R: And then, uh, she loosened up a little bit. She moved on to another Church, um, in the suburbs, a much larger Church. A little bit more open-minded, I'd have to say. But, uh, one of the things that really killed me was I was driving my nieces to the shopping mall, so at this point…nine years old, about. And she asks, me, "Auntie Jenny, have you taken Jesus Christ as your personal savior?"

Interviewer: Ha.

R: You know, where do you go with that? And I'm like, "No, sweetie, I'm sorry, I haven't. I…I really don't believe that."

Interviewer: Right.

R: And from the back seat in her sweet little voice, "Oh, Auntie Jenny, you're gonna go to Hell."

R: They've convinced my sweet, (*inaudible*) little nine-year-old niece that she would say that even?

Interviewer: They…

R: You know, that she would think that something to me as innocuous as that…

Interviewer: Mmm hmm.

R: …that means you're gonna go to Hell. I mean, if there's a Hell, I'm thinking you've got to do some pretty bad things…

Interviewer: Mmm hmm.

R: …to go to it, not not believe in something.

Interviewer: Mmm hmm.

R: You know? So…so, yeah, so my…my sister-in-law is…is still very much into her Church, though. They do go every Sunday, but it is a, to me, much less crazy Church, I guess. I guess I look at it that way. You know, when you think of, uh, you know, the whole idea of Bible thumping and…and whatever, you know, she was going to a Church like that and I just kept waiting for them to…to bring out the snakes, you know.

Interviewer: (*laughter*)

R: Um, but the new Church that they're going to, it's very friendly, um, much more community active, I would say.

R: Yeah. It…it's a nice Church. I mean, very nice people we met there and…and whatnot, but just not for me.

Interviewer: Right. And what about your brother?

R: I think he goes more because his wife kind of makes him go.

Interviewer: (*laughter*)

R: Yeah, I think he has discovered over the years that it is better to shut your mouth and go with your wife…

Interviewer: (*laughter*)

R: ...rather than have a big fight. Because he believes more along the lines of my mother...

Interviewer: Right.

R: ...and my sister, um, who are way more out there in their beliefs than I am. And, um, although it's interesting, I am finding that the longer he's married to her, the more, um, less open-minded he's becoming, which kind of makes me crazy, but...

Interviewer: In, uh, religion and/or (*inaudible*)...

R: Yeah. Yeah, about religion.

Interviewer: Mmm hmm.

R: Yeah, he...he's becoming more and more, um, I don't know, less liberal I guess they're thinking. I don't want to put it in terms of politics, but he's just...yeah, uh, he's just less open-minded than he used to be. I mean, I can say from, you know...I grew up with him...he used to believe in evolution. Now he doesn't.

Interviewer: Okay.

R: And I'm not quite sure how he backtracked there. You know, I see it as a backtrack. You know, I understand, you know, people believe what they want to believe and that's okay, but you know, I personally don't think that God put the dinosaurs there to trick us.

Interviewer: (*laughter*)

R: Or not trick us, I suppose, but to test us. Those were my sister-in-law's words.

Interviewer: (*laughter*)

R: You know, they're there to test us. I don't think so. So...

Interviewer: So when your parents, um, you know, were sort of thinking about leaving the Church and your whole family at some point left, um, was this happening gradually or, I mean, you know, even when you were holiday Catholics, was there one day when you all just sort of stopped going or...

R: You know...

Interviewer: ...you know, as a result you didn't go?

R: I remember vaguely going to Church a few more Sundays or so, maybe a couple months worth, after I made my communion. And then it was, well, we're not gonna go this weekend.

Interviewer: Mmm hmm.

R: And so it was a gradual thing, you know. And then it was, okay, well, we're gonna go for Easter. Okay, we would...we would go for Easter. We would go for Easter and...and, uh, Christmas. And then

Easter kind of fell out because it just...you know, we weren't getting anything out of it and it was, sadly to say, getting in the way of the Easter Egg hunt.

Interviewer: (*laughter*)

R: And, um, because you know, Easter Eggs, those have everything to do with Christ. And, um...and then we used to like to go to...to Christmas Mass, um, midnight Mass because we enjoyed it. We enjoyed the singing, we enjoyed the...the celebration of it and all of that. And then we kind of stopped doing that, too, because it was...it was getting in the way of...of our celebration of the holiday. So, see, here we are, we're lapsed Catholics, but we're still celebrating Christmas.

Interviewer: Mmm hmm.

R: You know, which is kind of goofy, but you know, because that's a big Christ holiday. Um, but again, I think we see the holidays more of, uh, a yearly family celebration than being particularly religious...

Interviewer: Mmm hmm.

R: ...now. You know, I think that that whole part...you know, when you start learning that the Catholics kind of stole Christmas from the Yule holiday and...and, you know, that a Christmas Tree's got nothing to do with that, you know, that that was a pagan thing and the...the decorating of it and this and that and all that other stuff, it kind of blows it for you.

Interviewer: Mmm hmm. Yeah.

R: You know what I mean? And...and the same thing happened with Easter, like I said. Eggs have what exactly to do with Christ and chocolate and...

Interviewer: Yeah, right.

R: You know, bunnies are for fertility and...and springtime and, you know, and Easter with a goddess, so what's that go to do with, you know, our supposed monotheism? You know, and when my mother really kind of got open to those things, it was somewhat, well, I don't know why we're bothering to go. We could play Christmas music at home because we...

R: You know, we kind of lost it because it just wasn't there for us. So we would play like music, oh good Lord. Did you hear me?

Interviewer: Yeah. (*laughter*):

R: Because we'd play the Christmas music at home or the holiday music. And, you know, I do kind of miss the community that we got with the Church.

Interviewer: Mmm hmm.

R: But the Church that we were going to in the town that we grew up in, even that started to feel very distant because, um, I don't know, I mean, I can't think of where…where those people were coming from. They had to be from the community, but I would go into Church and hardly recognize anybody.

***

Jenny finds the simple worldview of born again Christianity more vital and reassuring than the rigid religion of her childhood. Catholicism is dull and boring, all heavy and pointless theory, and stern controls. There is no freedom to live a simple life in God's love and salvation through Jesus. She does not understand why Mary has replaced Jesus in Catholicism. Like Julio, she is probably Puerto Rican and does not live in or near a Latino parish. She is not in any contact with Catholicism and does not seem to miss it very much. Like several other respondents she is alienated from her Catholic heritage and has practically speaking, no access to it. Fortunately for her personal life, this alternative provides her with a faith that brings happiness and love.

3. Eugenia

Interviewer 1: Um, like (*s/l Kelly*) said, what we're looking for is peoples' stories. (*inaudible*) what happened to you, how it felt, in our own words. So maybe just to start, could you tell us how your involvement with the Catholic Church changed, back all the way from your childhood until now?

R: How it changed?

Interviewer 1: Mmm-hmm.

Interviewer 2: Or if it has changed.

R: Well, yeah, it's changed. I, uh, think I said in the first interview that I went to Catholic schools from kindergarten through high school. And in high school, I had, you know, a really, um, raw experience. Because, um, I am sixty-two. So I was going through that civil rights era.

Interviewer 2: Mmm-hmm.

R: And, um, I, um, remember all the—I started to really pay attention to some of the really ugly things about racism.

Interviewer 2: Mmm-hmm.

R: And prejudice. That I never, you know, really thought about it, experienced before. Uh, because, you know, in the Catholic school, you had all white nuns, all white, you know, priests. And they all loved on you. And, you know, it was just that kind of place, you know. And then religion, of course, teaches you to love everybody.

Interviewer 2: Mmm-hmm.

R: I get to high school, and we got this whole different thing going on. I get kids walking around telling me stuff like, well, their parents told them that if they touch me, they're—they were—they were going to turn black. That I had kids in my gym class, um, wanting to see me change clothes because their parents told them I had a tail. And, you know, all of that was, you know, it got—it was kind of funny, you know, at the time, you know. Those things were kind of funny, until I got to a nun and—who told me she didn't want me to be president of her class because I was black. And from that point on, it was like all downhill. You know, because then I—I started to—to think to myself, well, all of these years have been a lie. That all the time the nuns were telling us that we're all equal, we're all loved, and all that stuff, you know, there they were, you know, just wanting what, my mom to spend her money to send me to a Catholic school, you know. And, uh, that all of that stuff about us being equal and all that stuff, you know. And then I started to kind of, you know, think to myself as a kid, you know, wait a minute, you know, I was really, really hurt. I mean, really hurt. And, um, from, um, the beginning of my jun—so—senior year, throughout my senior year, I refused religion classes. I absolutely refused to do it. Of course, I got an A, because, of course, the nun wasn't going to—to tell anybody why I refused to—to cooperate in her class, you know.

Interviewer 2: So she didn't want you to be president of your class?

R: Yeah.

Interviewer 2: Because you were black?

R: Yes.

Interviewer 2: And she told you that?

R: Yes.

Interviewer 2: Wow.

Interviewer 1: Um, during this time, were you also going to mass or (*inaudible-speaking simultaneously*)—?

R: I was still going to Church, because, um, I never told my mom. I never told my mom. I didn't—I didn't even know how to—I didn't know how to tell her, you know. And then I didn't know if, you know, because my mom was the kind of mom that said that if the nuns said something, you know, then that was it, you know. I don't care what you said, you didn't—there was no two-way street here. Whatever they said was it.

So I just ignored it, you know, I—I didn't—or at least I didn't tell my mom, I didn't ignore it, I just ignored the—the nun.

Interviewer 2: Mmm-hmm.

R: We were not taught at my house not to like you because you're white or pink or blue or whatever.

Interviewer 2: Mmm-hmm.

R: For somebody to tell you that, you know, was really kind of rough. Even though the kids running around saying that they were going to catch black, you know, it was kind of silly. So I—.

Interviewer 2: Mmm-hmm.

R: —just kind of overlooked that. And then that very same girl who wouldn't hold my hand, you know, from freshman year through senior year, at our graduation, you know, gave me the biggest hug you ever saw in your life, you know, because she realized, you know, like I did, like I knew from when I was a kid that there's no such thing, there's no difference between us except the color of our skin.

Interviewer 2: Mmm-hmm.

R: And that's what we were all taught. That's what she was taught. And as we moved through school. And then as she saw this whole dynamics of what happened in our homeroom, because she was in my homeroom, and she and I had—her last name started—started with G-z or something, and mine was H-a. So we were always next to each other.

Interviewer 2: Mmm-hmm.

R: And I used to say silly stuff to her like, "Don't touch me. You're trying to steal my black."

Interviewer 2: Mmm-hmm. (*laughter*)

R: You know, that kind of—you know, just, you know, because we—we lived like that for years. And finally, graduation she came up and she says, "I'm going to miss you." And I said, "No, you're not." She says, "Yes, I am." And she went to hug me. I said, "Are you going to try to steal my black again?' And she just grabbed me and hugged me.

Interviewer 2: Mmm-hmm.

R: And that was—the only thing that kind of eased my whole—eased that whole thing for me.

Interviewer 2: Mmm-hmm.

R: You know. Because it was like all this time, I didn't know. I really, truly did not understand that whole thing.

Interviewer 2: Were there other black kids in the school?

R: Uh, yes. Um, that school at the time was approximately 10 percent black.

Interviewer 2: Okay.

R: So there weren't very many of us, but there were a few.

Interviewer 1: What happened after graduation?

R: After graduation, because I had to go from mass to Sunday school all my life, I kind of drifted, you know. I was still living at home. When I still lived at home, I had to go to mass. I still had to go to Church every Sunday. Um, wasn't getting very much out of it. I just went because that—it was just routine and that's what we had to do. And, um, then as I got older, I didn't go.

Interviewer 1: Mmm-hmm.

R: Until, uh, my daughter was born and I decided to have her baptized. And because I'd been Catholic all my life, I thought, well, you know, my mom was still going to Church, going to Catholic Church. Even though I don't think my mom became a Catholic until, God, I was in high school or something. You know, or until after I graduated, as a matter of fact, until my sister went to school, to high school. So, um, she still went. And I had my daughter baptized in a Catholic Church. But I didn't take her very often.

Interviewer 1: Mmm-hmm.

Interviewer 1: Was your mother going to a different Church?

R: Um, my mom was going to both. She was going to—to Catholic Church because we were there. And she was going to the Church my grandfather was, uh, uh, was a deacon in, which is why we had to go to mass and Sunday school.

Interviewer 1: And what Church was that?

R: Uh, I think it was an Apostolic Church at the time.

Interviewer 1: So you went to both Churches?

R: Yes.

Interviewer 1: Okay. And then your mom converted (*inaudible-speaking simultaneously*)—?

R: I think my mom converted like later on.

Interviewer 2: Mmm-hmm.

R: You know, because she still goes.

Interviewer 1: Okay.

R: As a matter of fact.

Interviewer 1: Is there any particular reason?

R: Any particular reason she still goes?

Interviewer 1: Or she converted? She switched?

R: Uh, I don't know. Probably because, you know, I guess she got older and started to settle in (*laughter*), you know. And I guess the same thing that I've done, you know, as I got older, I settled in and decided I wanted to be in a Church.

Interviewer 1: Uh-huh. And you were living at home for most of this time?

R: No, I was, um, the time I got my degree, I was married—.

Interviewer 2: Mmm-hmm.

R: —as a matter of fact. I was married and, um, I had, um, one baby. And, um, my son was born like five months before I got my degree, as a matter of fact.

Interviewer 1: Okay. And you started going to Church again when you were—?

R: No, not really. I just went sporadically.

Interviewer 1: Okay.

Interviewer 2: Mmm-hmm.

R: I went sporadically.

Interviewer 1: Um, on the survey, you put down you belong to the Apostolic Church now?

R: Yes. It's really a nondenominational kind of Church.

Interviewer 2: Mmm-hmm.

R: And, um, I started going to another—I started going to Church after I really kind of messed up my life a little bit. And needed something to kind of keep me from going off the deep end. And, um, I picked a Church that, uh, my godmother was going to, because her son was a dynamic, dynamic preacher and had, you know, some really soothing things to say.

Interviewer 1: Mmm-hmm.

R: The Church, however, was a little too run by the people. You know, I mean, it's like—.

Interviewer 2: Hmm.

R: —you got a Church where everybody runs it but the pastor.

Interviewer 1: Mmm-hmm.

Interviewer 2: Mmm-hmm.

R: You know, and they're all, you know, kind of petty. So I thought this is not for me. And then I found this Church. And where the pastor is very dynamic and is into real life kind of thing. And even though I grew up in the Bible, in the Catholic Church, you never really read it the way—the way that—that he presented it, you know. Even though I remember the passages and stuff, it's just that I guess I—I—when I listened to him, I thought, I never understood that, you know. And he explains it. And I think what drove me to his Church is that he said there's no sense going to Church if it doesn't help you live your life. If you can't...

Interviewer 2: Excuse me one second. I'm sorry.

R: —you can't function from day to day.

Interviewer 1: Mmm-hmm.

R: With what we're—with what I'm preaching to you on a Sunday afternoon—.

R: That's the kind of preaching that he does. He—he shows you. He said, "If I can't show you in the Bible, don't believe me." He said, "And in the Bible it tells you, you know, you can't do this and you can't do that. And it says that right there."

Interviewer 1: Mmm-hmm. So when you do do that—?

R: You—unless you're—unless you're really, um, uh, playing—playing Church or playing—playing Christian, then you have a tendency to have a serious conscience thing going on. (*laughter*) You know, a serious, "Oh, God, please forgive me," you know, kind of thing going on. Which, you know, you know, it's on a—and he says on a—and he's very real. He says, "On a regular, everyday basis, I have to repent." He says, "Because I get angry. I want to cuss. I want to slap somebody," you know (*laughter*), he says so. He said—says, "Nothing wrong with you're thinking that. But then it is something wrong if you don't go back and say, 'God, I'm sorry. I know that's not how I'm supposed to behave.'"

Interviewer 1: Mmm-hmm.

R: You know, just sometimes I thought to myself, "You just think too deeply about stuff," you know. And, um, finding, you know, finding God again, you know, at least have—well, having God found me again. Saying to me, "It's not that bad. You don't need, uh, you don't need the pills."

***

I blush at this horrible story. I know the neighborhood and the school. Eugenia is not exaggerating. It was steeped in racism of the most virulent variety. She was driven from the Church by her white classmates and the nuns. She was doubtless an idealistic young woman who worshiped the nuns and was enthralled by the Church. If she depends on pills, as she tells us at the end of the interview, it is easy to suspect that here teenage experience is part of the problem. So too it is probably partially responsible for her life problems she mentions later. She would have grown up to be the kind of intensely Catholic African American matron that one often encounters in black parishes. The nuns who tormented her are gone, the school no longer exists, yet the harm it did continues. Most nuns of course are not racists—or if they are they are too smart become explicit about it. They were probably tormented by doubts about their behavior that were parallel to Eugenia's. This is not the only story we will hear about the negative impact of priests and nuns on young people in Catholic schools. One wants to say that these incidents are not typical, but that they were and are totally unacceptable. How many young men and women have been driven away by such oppression? And yet Eugenia did have her daughter baptized. Then she found in Fundamentalism the faith and love she needed and had lost.

4. James

R: My history with the Church. I went to Catholic school when I—up until fourth grade. And, uh, of course that's childhood experiences, not—not anything that I thought that much about when I did it. It was just something that—that you did as a matter of course. So you went—you went to Church. After—after the fourth grade, uh, for reasons not my own, we—we switched to public school. And I kind of just quit going to Church.

Interviewer 2: That was in—how old were you when you quit going to Church?

R: Probably ten.

Interviewer 1: Was your family—were—were—did you regularly attend mass prior to that—you know, that fourth grade, you know, during that period, were you—was your family involved in the Church?

R: They were not involved, no. We would occasionally attend Mass.

Interviewer 1: Okay. Um, did you go for, um, was it like holidays or was it strictly just for the—the gathering type events?

R: No, it would have been more holy—what do you mean, gathering type—?

Interviewer 1: Um, um, weddings and funerals, sir.

R: No, now I do. And now I'll once—it's been a while, but I'll sometime go Easter, Christmas, if it's a social thing where—where we're going. Uh, we're—my family is—my current family, uh, is getting together to go, I might do that. But when I was, uh, when I was practicing as a child, you know, going now and then, that was it.

Interviewer 1: Okay.

Interviewer 2: Okay. And now—.

R: Also, of course, when I was in a Catholic school, we had—we went in the morning and often, before we started school, I was—there was a Church right in the school.

Interviewer 2: Okay. Um, well, you said you occasionally attend now. Um, is that—that's only for holidays?

R: Yes, it would be a social thing, not a religious thing.

Interviewer 2: And is your family Catholic or were you married in the Catholic Church?

R: Uh, no, I was never married in the Catholic Church. Well, my—my wife is Catholic, but she really isn't practicing now, either. She practiced well into her life and worked with the Church, too, with youth groups and things. But she doesn't right now.

Interviewer 1: When—when you were going to school, to Catholic school, did you, um, did you receive any of the sacraments? Did you, um, were you baptized and did you ever receive communion?

R: We went there—at the time when I—when I was a child, you were baptized just after you were born.

Interviewer 1: Okay.

R: And I was baptized. But I—and I had communion, but I dropped out before confirmation.

Interviewer 1: Okay. Okay.

Interviewer 2: And, um, what are your strongest memories from your childhood in the Catholic school or at the Church with your family?

R: At the school? Uh, my strongest memory—memories really were kind of being bullied by the nuns.

Interviewer 2: So they were not the best teachers?

R: I wouldn't say they weren't the best teachers. I said—I was talking about being bullied by them. I thought they—they were tough. And I think—I think they were sometimes just—just rough on—rough on me. But that—that's—that's a little kid. And look—looking back on it, some of the stuff I think it's rather surprising that—that someone who's supposed to be a teacher would be that rough with a kid. But I wouldn't say they weren't good teachers, because when I did come out of there, whether I was—whether I was a smart kid or not, when I got to the public school, I was a—rather an academic star.

Interviewer 2: Mmm-hmm.

Interviewer 1: Were the—was the punishment harsh or was it just the criticism or was there something about them specifically that, uh, that you didn't like?

R: What I didn't like? I wouldn't say punishment was—was harsh. I thought they were—just being treated unfairly. I remember a couple of times when I—when I stood up there, you know, a nun is just yelling in my face because something had happened which really wasn't my, you know, that I really wasn't at fault at. And then because I didn't crack, in fact, I always remember that to this day, her yelling at me, "You are a bold one, aren't you?" And I'm thinking to myself at the time, "What are you talking, bold, you know? I'm—I'm very frightened right now." But, uh, but I'm not cracking.

Interviewer 1: Were the priest like this, as well, or was it just the experiences that you had with the nuns?

R: No, the—the priests—the priests were always, um, likeable fellows, I have to say, but we did not have a lot of interaction with the—with the—with the priests.

Interviewer 1: Yeah, how did it make you feel about the Church itself, those experiences?

R: You know, even as a child, I somewhat didn't look at the nuns as being the Church. Even though I—I had—I had had those, you know, some unpleasant experiences in the, uh, in—in school with them. Uh, even—even as a child, I didn't—I didn't count those as—as the Church. You know, at that time, was—I wasn't that heavy-duty a practicing, uh, Catholic, as a matter of fact. I remember one thing they had, which looking—even at the time, I thought was not a—a decent thing to do to a child. When we were in third grade or fourth grade there, we had a thing where it was an army and it depended on, you know, we—they treated us as—they had this—this program. And it was like an army, and for wh—and the masses you attended and so, such and such, you raised up in rank. And, uh, I didn't—I didn't go that—that much on Sunday to mass and things. So I didn't rise up in rank very well. And they did give me a dishonorable discharge. And I remember at the time, even as a child, it didn't bother me that much, but I could think of myself, I said, "This is a rotten thing to do to a kid." You know, they're making me feel bad about this. Uh, and I think that that was probably again—again, looking back on it, one of the reasons we prob.—another reason we probably went to the public schools, is I really wasn't fitting in there, because I was not a practicing Catholic even in, you know, even as a ten-year-old. And our family wasn't. We—my—the parents had sent me to the Catholic school more because it was a superior school than, uh, than for the religious aspects of it. That's true today, too.

Interviewer 2: You mentioned dishonorable—.

R: (*inaudible*) today, because I don't go to school. But people do go to Catholic schools because they want their children to be in better schools, not because they want them to be particularly religious.

Interviewer 1: Did you—I'm unfamiliar with this—this—the army, this—this idea, you know, I've never heard of this before. Um, could you elaborate more on it, like the system or what—what was the expectations they had for you or—or for the children?

R: Well, no, the more—the more you went to masses, and I don't remember what it was besides masses, I think that was about it, the more you moved up in rank. It was just, uh, because—because you have a—because you have a hierarchy in an army, you could move up from a private to a corporal to a sergeant, depending on, you know, up to—I suppose if you went to Church three times a day, you could become a lieutenant general. And—and it was just, uh, a way—a way of measuring your—your attendance.

R: I get what you're talking about. Uh, the Catholic Church is a hierarchical organization, I know that, and I knew that when I was a—I don't know when I—when I first knew that. But, uh, it's no big—big philo—there was no big philosophical thing about that when—in my life. That's the way it is, a lot of organizations are like that, most are.

Interviewer 1: Okay. Did you have any other brothers and sisters, sir?

R: Yes.

Interviewer 1: Did they go to, uh, the Catholic schools, as well?

R: Well, my brother went for two years.

Interviewer 1: Okay.

R: When I—when I went for four, he went for two.

Interviewer 1: Okay. Okay.

R: And he was really doing poorly there. That was one of the main reasons I believe we left for the public school. My parents thought that—that he would do better in—in the public school.

Interviewer 1: —we discussed before that the Catholic schools have a more strict regimen of, you know—.

R: Yeah.

Interviewer 1: —academics. But was it about the not fitting in, because you weren't necessarily regular practicing—?

R: I think—I think that that was—I don't know how much of a consideration that was for me. For him, it was the—the atmosphere, the discipline, he did—did not take to that.

Interviewer 1: Okay.

R: Well, I didn't either. They say I was bold though, I knew when I was frightened or could be bullied but I—I could handle it.

Interviewer 1: Okay.

R: And he was more overtly reb—rebellious about—in that way. He also was not a good student. And I don't know, uh, he—he wasn't a good student, so he had a bad time in school that way, too.

Interviewer 2: Well, would you have, for yourself, would you have preferred to stay in the Catholic school or were you happy going to the public school after that?

R: I was happy going to the public school.

Interviewer 1: Do you have children yourself, sir?

R: Yes, I have children.

Interviewer 1: Um, do you raise them in the Catholic Church or—?

R: No, I didn't raise them as—as—with any, uh, religious upbringing really.

Interviewer 1: Okay.

R: I raised them morally. And, uh, the two of them don't belong to any Church. My son—other son is very much into his Church.

Interviewer 1: And you said that you occasionally go to masses now—.

R: Weddings and funerals and sometimes for a social thing, it will be Christmas and/or Easter and we'll go there, you know, that—that's it.

Interviewer 1: Is it, um, do you feel like an obligation or is it—is there something that's, um, soothing about it or not soothing? Or are there things that kind of bring back bad memories? Or how do you feel when you're at the events?

R: Um, I don't feel bad about it. It—it's something that I—that I—that I watch going on and I listen to them. Uh, you know, so it's not a bad feeling thing. Funerals aren't usually too good.

Interviewer 1: Yes. Yeah. (*laughter*)

R: But, uh, does this—I have no particular feelings about a mass. I like—I like to—I hate to say this, I shouldn't hate to say anything though, but just the spectacle of it is interesting to me, once in a while like that, to—to watch it and participate in it, to the extent that I participate. It's not like when I was a kid and getting dragged to it. You know, going, it—it's quite a fancy thing. In fact, for the fanciness, I really preferred Latin.

R: But I don't know, I thought the Latin—the—the Latin mass has got that ritual to it that I—I thought that maybe it's because I—I went to Mass as, you know, as a child, I think that that's—that's more in fitting with, uh, with—with a Mass. You shouldn't have to understand what it is. You can't understand those words anyhow.

R: And I listen—and I listen to—to the priest talk. And when they're talking about moral issues and—and even religious issues, those—those are serious things. And I—I should—I don't say I—I obviously, if I really liked it, I'd be going more to it on my own. But when I'm there, I don't object to it.

Interviewer 1: So would you ever, um, have you ever thought of considering going back to the Church or becoming more of an active member or?

R: Uh, no.

Interviewer 1: Is there anything behind that decision? Is it a—a moral decision or is it just you not think about it or? Is there anything—maybe I should put it this way. Is there anything particularly that holds you back from attending?

R: Um, I just don't care about it.

Interviewer 1: About the Church or about religion in general?

R: About—about both.

Interviewer 1: Okay.

Interviewer 2: So you would characterize your experience with the cat—Catholicism as a—an appreciation for ritual, uh, but not necessarily accompanied by the deep belief?

R: Right. Of course, when you're a child, you believe in—you know, you're hearing this and you're believing in—in God as God is represented in the Church. And, uh, well, that's what it is when you're a child. And I was a child when I was in there. So my—there's -there's belief as—as a child. In fact, there's a belief—there's a belief all the time. But I—except I don't—I don't—and I don't know if you guys are asking about this or care about it or not, this whole notion of God the Creator or of Jesus Christ as the Son of God is something that I just plain don't know about. And I don't feel uncomfortable not knowing about it.

R: And as far as dogma goes, that—that's a necessary thing for an organized religion. I don't have anything against that. And if somebody—somebody accepts it, that's—that's fine with me. I just—I don't.

Interviewer 2: So is there anything else about the Church that you maybe don't approve of or dislike or are a little uncomfortable with? Specifically the Catholic Church.

R: Oh. That I'm uncomfortable with or I don't approve of? I—there's a lot of things people—I do—don't approve of that aren't a big deal. And generally, the social policies of the Church and the politics of it is something that I—that I generally, when I hear them, it's not what I believe.

I see the Church take one side in it, that is that, okay, everybody is welcome, and you certainly can be welcome in a Church, doesn't mean you have to be welcome in the country. And the politics are usually what you call left wing politics.

R: The economics that you hear comings—that I hear coming from the Church. And I'm going to be maybe hard-pressed to get a specific thing, but it's generally a socialist thing, that collect more taxes, do more for the people. And you don't do for the people when you have an economic system that—that is in decline. I mean, here, look at—look at the difference between un—that's—that's I guess what I—.

Interviewer 1: Um, sir, do you have anything else you'd like to add? Is there anything that kind of comes to your mind when people say the Catholic Church to you? Or any kind of final thoughts?

R: Thoughts when people say the Catholic Church to me?

Interviewer 1: Yes, sir. What kind of connotations come to your mind? Or what do you think about? Or?

R: I just—I just think about the nice buildings, the services, and so forth. That—that's my basic, uh, thing that—that I think about. And the Catholic Church, for the most part, is giving people who have the belief, uh, positive, uh, aspects in their life and support in certain things. And that—that's—that's fine with me.

Interviewer 1: Um, I think—.

R: (*inaudible-speaking simultaneously*) the Church. I—I—don't get me wrong. I—overall, I look at it as a positive organization.

Interviewer 1: It sounds like you—your—your final thoughts were that—that, you know, you have a positive perspective on the Church?

R: Yeah, and a lot of things I don't like. But I do have a positive perspective on it. It's—it's—of—of all the things in the world, all the organizations, as far as actually advancing the welfare of humanity, the—they're up there.

Interviewer 1: The Catholic Church or like organized religion, in general?

R: Well, organized religion in—uh, when I think of religion, I'm still enough, you know, from my—my childhood, I think of Catholic as—as the primo one.

Interviewer 1: So you do give the—the Catholic Church credit for advancing let's say human condition. I hate to, you know, sound corny or something but—.

R: Today? Yes, I do. I do. When we—when we go back to John Paul and, uh, he—he was one of the people who stood up to the Soviets and that certainly advanced the—the human condition. The stuff that went down in Poland that was—was a big advance for—for people. And he—and I don't know where the rest of the Churches stood on that, but the Catholic Church was—was—was in the forefront of really freeing a lot of—freeing people up in Eastern Europe.

Interviewer 1: I think we kind of, uh, rather than just asking peoples' opinions on like specific issues, we see if we kind of—if that's when we say, do you have positive or negative connotations about the Church and those type of things, is this something that's so salient to you that you'll bring it up.

R: Oh, okay.

Interviewer 1: You know?

R: No, it isn't. Because I think it's for the most part a bum rap. That there's a certain—it was not a bum rap that they didn't get on top of it.

Interviewer 1: Uh—.

R: That's the rap. But as far as deviant people in the priesthood as well as everybody else, there's going to be a small number of them. And probably a smaller number there than in society in general.

Interviewer 2: Mmm-hmm.

R: So that's not a salient issue for me. But that's the one—if you—if you do watch television or pass by one now and then, see the news, that's—that's the big—the big rap. And I—I think perhaps that's a—that's another thing. When I—when you do see most information about the Church in the news media, it's negative.

Interviewer 1: So it seems like you're saying this really isn't an issue for you because you think they're getting a bad rap?

R: It—it's not a big issue for me vis-à-vis the Church. And I think they're getting a—a bad rap in—in—in—yeah, that's all you hear about if—those Churches, this pedophilia thing. And there's, uh, I don't think they're any worse than anybody else. Now, since they're in a position of being—supposed to be moral leaders, that gives the—of course, the hypocrisy issue comes up because of that and it makes them more vulnerable to a bad rap, but it still is a bad rap, for the most part.

R: How would I know that, who you're working for? You told me and I believed you.

Interviewer 1: Okay. But if you didn't believe us, you could call this number and check us out basically.

Interviewer 2: Yeah—.

R: I mean, if you turn out to be the Communists or somebody—.

Interviewer 1: (laughter) No, no. I promise.

R: No, we're good. We're good.

Interviewer 1: Okay. Great, sir. Alright. Enjoy the weekend. And thank you very much for speaking with us.

R: You, too. Thank you. Bye bye.

***

James is another one of the lost sheep who had problems with nuns, though not of the tragic dimensions that tormented Eugenia's life. He concedes that they were good teachers. He respects the work that the Church does and rises to its defense against what he considers to be bad raps. He decries sexual abuse by priests but understands how it can happen and thinks that the media give a "bad rap." He is impressed with what the Church accomplished in Eastern Europe but disapproves of the "socialism" of the Church's political involvement in this country, which seems to him to be "socialism." He casts himself as a tolerant and educated man who makes sensible and balanced judgment. So he doesn't hate the nuns but didn't particularly like their harshness.

The incidents he describes recall to me one of the great failures in my life, or so seemed to me then and so it seems now. A nun screamed at a girl in my sixth grade class. She lived down the street from us and I had a crush on her. She wasn't very bright, though more likely she was shy and from a troubled family. The nun demanded that she answer a question and the girl was silent, either because she didn't know the answer or because she was frightened and humiliated. Tears streamed down her face. The nun screamed repeatedly that she was a "bold stump." We were all silent, embarrassed for our friend, and afraid to rise to her defense. We had walked to school together for six years. I was as silent as everyone else. I never did apologize. This same emotionally troubled nun compulsively hit our fingers with a yardstick ruler that she carried like it was a weapon of mass destruction. My handwriting was (and is) terrible. I escaped my fate for months because I was destined for the seminary. But one lovely spring morning she went after my fingers because I was holding my pencil improperly (a valid charge). The hapless pencil flew out of my hand. She denounced me as a "bold stump." I reported the adventure that night.

My father appeared at the rectory door that night and demanded that this behavior stop at once. The ruler was not there the next day and the poor nun was gone in a week. I was so proud of my dad—and in retrospect ashamed of myself that I had not taken Sister on. I hope in the world to come that I get a chance to apologize to my love of so long ago. Now I understand how difficult convent life must have been for many women and how deeply troubled they became. I don't know what happened to the girl down the street. I never spoke to her after the classroom incident and never saw her after graduation. I gather that she had a difficult life. I can't blame the sixth-grade nun for that. And I don't blame nuns and priests for driving young people out of Church. Most of us follow the path which James did. We worshipped the "good" ones and bracketed the "bad" ones. We celebrate their dedication and decry the system that drove some of them to their wit's end. In fact, the class drove the sixth-grade teacher out of the classroom, aided by my dad and the Monsignor. Beside those two, there are no heroes in this brief memoir. To be fair to my classmates, we disposed of five other teachers that year.

5. Patricia

Phone interview, started late (originally scheduled for 7:30) because R was out running errands. We had some trouble using the phones, with VR/JM dropping R once trying to transfer to speaker, and R switching out phones to hear better.

JM starts with "How has your involvement with the Catholic Church changed?" R now only attends family functions: "my family is still Catholic, so any communion, baptism, um, you know, that sort of thing." In follow-up, R reports that her family lives in Chicago, and that she doesn't go to Mass with them.

VR asks about R's new Church and her decision to leave. R: "Yeah, sure, you know I didn't find the Catholic Churches to be...very...informative? (*inflected like a question*). Half the time I didn't really know, uh I mean I knew what was going on, but there isn't really any type of preaching[?] or teaching[?], um, a lot kinda follow the same exact...um...you know, schedule[?]...I was, I was just not getting anything out of mass."

JM asks about her current Church: "It's a lot more involving...its more informative, I just learn a lot more...I understand the Bible better, so you know they go through a verse and then they explain what it means—then you know how to apply it, that sort of thing. It's sort of like a Church-slash, you know, -theology class."

VR asks if the switch to the new Church was gradual or sudden: "It was a sudden shift...I had never really attended Presbyterian Church before, but then somebody invited me, and I really liked it, I liked the music, and I liked the...you know I had already had some sort of issues with the entire Catholic teaching[?]...like I think I talked about it in my first interview, that I'm not entirely sure that I believe in, you know, the pope, who he is, and that sort of thing...and just mass in general, I wasn't learning anything."

JM asks about current practices besides attending sermons: "We do, well, we used to, I just had a baby so now it's a little bit more difficult, so when the baby was born we were attending a weekly bible study group."

VR asks about her spouse and if R's decision was affected by her spouse's religion: "You know, I think it was the other way around, when I, um, well, we had broken up and then I was already going to the Church and so he kinda attended because of me, it was equal for him, he really liked it as well." VR follows up, and we learn that the husband was from a Catholic home but not active in practice.

VR asks about memories of the Catholic Church growing up: "Our parents didn't really push it on us, so I attended on my own will, really, when I was a little bit older. I remember...I remember my communion, my communion lasted, but I don't remember anything they taught me, I was really young, you know there are problems now because the kids are too young at that age, as far as I know I don't remember anything from that age...I do remember it being very boring, as a child, not really grasping what was going on."

JM asks about attending communions of family members, now: "Well, now, I'm a lot more attuned, I do know, I know the meaning of it, so it's a lot more entertaining and meaningful...to me, just because I study the Bible more and the truth behind it and how important it is, so there is a lot more..."

VR asks about pageantry, R doesn't understand question at first, but says she still enjoys the pageantry. VR asks about Christmas and Easter, R says she does Christmas Mass with her sisters and Good Friday at her own Church.

JM asks about the family's reaction to the new Church: "Most of them are ok, they sometimes like going there too, because they have a children's study, kids enjoy it a lot more, um, so its not a hassle to take them to Church on Sunday because they have fun there, with the other kids, but my oldest sister had a problem with that. They don't consider it an actual...religion—anything outside of Catholicism they don't consider an actual, you know real."

JM asks about friends and neighbors: "I made a lot of friends at my new Church, those are my current, but I also have another set of friends that are still Catholic."

On follow up, R reveals that she talks about religion with her Presbyterian friends, but seldom with her Catholic friends, for them religion is more private: "its not necessarily a way of everyday life for them."

R sums up her reasons for leaving the Church: issues with the teachings and issues with the service.

VR asks for clarification about beliefs and practices, R lists the three beliefs she had trouble with as "how they glorify the pope...the saints..." JM asks about the Virgin Mary: "She's Jesus' mother, a very important person in the Catholic theology, but I don't pray to her."

VR asks about prayer: "Prayer itself, quiet time, I do it less, but in the morning, definitely, and in the evenings, and I would say throughout the day I'm constantly, in prayer." VR asks about her prayer as a Catholic: "It was definitely a lot less." JM asks if R has a different style of prayer now: "Definitely more frequent, even as a Catholic I never prayed to saints, maybe when I was a lot younger and that was what I was taught, but as soon as I got old enough to understand different, I definitely didn't." JM asks about "Hail Mary's" and "Our Father's": "I definitely do, when I do Mass, but definitely not, as personal prayers to God." VR asks and R confirms that she mostly prays to Jesus.

VR asks about "essentially Catholic beliefs:" the Eucharist, help for the poor, etc: "Absolutely...that hasn't changed...The one thing I personally really like about Catholicism is the fact that priests don't get married, that they give their entire lives to Jesus, I think there's a lot to say for that, that's a big plus...so, there's still a lot of things about Catholicism I still really like, um...I absolutely feel that, in order to serve God the best, you really have to not be married, because then that takes priority over your life."

JM asks about priests R has met: "The priest at the one Church that I used to attend, the one that probably got the closest to, um, the preaching-teaching type of service that I really enjoyed...I never met him personally. But I really liked him, I saw him every Sunday, he was really good, that Church did a lot of mission work."

VR asks what R misses: "I do miss the Church setting, the actual setting. Our Church, the Church is held in an auditorium of a music school, so that took a lot of getting used to, because it's not a traditional setting. I do miss the actual Church, the architecture, the feeling of holiness when you come into this big place."

VR asks whether it is important that the Church provides a sense of community: "Yeah...I didn't get that in the Catholic Church, I never made any friends there, you know, I never really met the priest, I guess you could try to get more involved…but the Presbyterian Churches I've been to have definitely been more welcoming, more personal…"

JM asks about fellowship activities: "There are picnics, we're all friends, so we do a lot of new-comer welcome parties, not parties but, um, you know brunches, that sort of thing…(clicks while thinking)…that's pretty much it, we all go out to brunch after Church every Sunday. We have a bunch of classes, not just Bible study, they have lots of different ones, one of the most interesting ones was just a review, a study on Revelations, that one focused a lot on the second coming, the other one I was on 'how to read your Bible,' the other one that I did was just an entire course on Grace."

JM asks what particular stories R enjoys: "I know the one story I do love is David, because I read an entire book on his life story."

VR asks about R raising her child Presbyterian: "Well, basically, I just want it to be a part of her life, not just a Sunday thing. The way that I was brought up it was, you believe in God, this is the way that it is, but I didn't really know what that meant, so I knew there was a God, I didn't really know how I should relate to him, so there was really no teaching involved. So, I want that to be completely different for my child, I want it to be something really good, something she can hold on to, I want it to be her priority, something she can run to, whenever something happens, because I was never really brought up that way, that's not the way that my nieces and nephews are being brought up, they're all being baptized, they're all going to their communions, but none of their parents enforce any type of teachings on them, so they don't necessarily take them to Church every Sunday, they don't…they don't follow through with prayer at night, or prayer in the morning, or anything like that, its not, you would not find them in part of their everyday vocabulary, ever. And that's the way I was brought up, and I don't want that for Sophia."

JM follows up on specific practices: "Just always be grateful, you know, to always know that God is in her life, just having that sense of God, just having it as part of her life, everyday life, that he's always there…" JM: "You mentioned prayer in the morning, prayer at night…" R: "Yeah, hopefully I can follow through on that, yeah I believe that in the morning when you wake up first thing you should do is remember, and at night, and also throughout the day."

VR asks about family practice vs. individual practice: "No, I want it to be a family…I would never pray with my parents…it was always a very private thing, I want her to be open, about that."

JM asks about R's nieces and nephews going to Church with her: "They do stories, they also do, you know, art projects that involve a particular story, they play games…you know…" JM asks about time: "Its every Sunday, every Sunday there's child service, at one point in the sermon all the children go, and the adults stay to hear the sermon."

VR asks R about taking her to family Catholic practices: "Absolutely…if she in her heart wants to be Catholic, like, um, she can. At the end of the day, I think its about God, and there's subtle differences, between any Christian group anyway, maybe if she converts to Judaism, um, if she wants to go to a Catholic Church she has every right…my priority is that she is a practicing Catholic, and not just your Sunday, Christmas day goer."

VR follows up, asking whether exposed R's daughter to Catholicism is a way of connecting her to her family. R agrees.

VR follows up about one of R's sisters not being happy about her leaving the Catholic Church: "She didn't really go to Church herself, so for most of our family, being Catholic is just part of being Mexican, so she's not necessarily, I wouldn't say she's a practicing Catholic, you know her kids are not, she doesn't take her kids to Church, she doesn't necessarily teach them anything about Catholicism…for her, if you're not Catholic, then really there is no other…for example, when we were getting married, we were getting married in a Presbyterian Church, and for her it was not a valid marriage…She's the only one who hasn't been to my Church…She might go for the baby's christening, but that's it."

VR follows up about the Catholic/Mexican identity connection: "That's basically it, its part of who you are, so many traditions that are involved in it, that you were brought up with, so no one really can distinguish what is Catholic and what is Mexican…so that's why there's still a lot of things that I do, a lot of traditions I still hold on to, you know Good Friday, Lent."

JM asks about crises involving this identity and switching to the Presbyterian Church: "I did have a hard time because I felt like I was trained, who I was brought up to be in my family, but I got over it. I understood the difference between the two. I'm still a good person."

VR about Mexican friends in the new Church, and R replies that her Church is predominately Korean.

Patricia is a "fallen away Catholic who doesn't think that she's really fallen away. She is still Mexican and is inclined to think that her sister is right that to be Mexican is to be Catholic. There are many

Churches perhaps, but Catholicism is the oldest and the best, even if her sister doesn't take her children to Church and doesn't go herself . . . Patricia's own story is that she always was a Catholic and still is and that she became Presbyterian because the man she loved insisted on it. She reports that her sister almost did not come to the wedding because it wasn't a Catholic wedding. Neither sister has anything against Catholicism though Patricia has formally left it but still defines herself as Catholic and her sister, who doesn't think Patricia is Catholic because she is not married in Church, doesn't practice. Their story illustrates the problems and confusions of Mexican Americans who are generally flexible about moving across denominational lines and still have Catholic loyalties even if at the moment they happen to have other affiliations. One wonders if a sympathetic priest who understands might have found a way out of this dilemma.

6. Sean

The recorder was full and because I didn't want to erase anything, opted to just take notes.

R is in his late fifties and lives in a unique home in [*city*]. As I walked in and introduced myself, he immediately began talking about the renovation work he was undertaking on the home and what a labor of love it was, especially since he is an "anal worker" and likes everything to be "just so." Because it is a Frank Lloyd Wright house, there are many quirks—it looks good, but not the best engineering—this makes it even more difficult. He offered me coffee and we sat in the kitchen eating nook for the interview.

R explained that he knew [*person*] through his wife, who was [*person's*] roommate in graduate school. He was very curious about this research and enjoyed participating in the survey and was looking forward to the follow-up. I went over the IRB material, explaining confidentiality, etc. He asked more about how I knew [*person*] and asked about NORC and the relationship to the Survey Lab. I explained that [*person*] is on the board of the Lab and that he was involved in the sampling of the survey portion of the study. We talked a bit more about my role at the Lab and the course. I explained that since I live in [*city*] I did not bring a student with me. We talked a bit about [*city*], and then about R's time in [*neighborhood*]. He is an extended grad student in the geography department, which doesn't exist anymore. He is still working on his dissertation. He works from home and has a wife with two adopted kids, ages eight and two. (*There were no kids in the house that I could hear or see while I was there*). He apologized for noise as there was a man in the house working on the alarm system. Finally, we started the interview.

I asked R to talk about his strongest memories of the Catholic Church. He took a while to respond and said, "well, I'll tell you the first thing that pops into my mind. that's vague, but it keeps coming back as I try to remember...the tedium of it all. I just think of myself in Church, being bored. I guess I remember my first communion, sort of." I asked if there was something specific about the first communion he remembered and he couldn't recall. He did say that he had his confirmation very shortly after the first communion—just a few years (*this was something new for me; I always knew confirmation to take place in 7th or 8th grade and first communion in 1st or 2nd grade. For him it was just a few years apart*).

R explained that his family is mostly Irish and immigrated to the US two generations ago. His first marriage was in the Catholic Church, but this was to a Lutheran woman from Germany. He grew up going to Church every week. He attended Catholic school through the 8th grade, when his family moved and he could not continue. He was upset about this but mostly because he was going to now be away from his friends. He said that his father thought one could "over do a Catholic education." I asked him what he meant by this, and he said that he was never really sure, but assumed it might have something to do with "developing independent thought."

I asked R about his feelings about Catholicism growing up beyond the tedium he described. He described a sort of passive acceptance, it was "what you did" but there was a lack of connection for him. They continued to go to Church in his new town, where he described the parish as an "enterprise," and the pastor as "money grubbing." Apparently, the Church developed in a converted supermarket while they raised money to build a proper Church. He never did attend that built Church until his father died.

When R went to college, he started off going to Church every Sunday. One Sunday in the spring of his first year, he stopped going to Mass. One day he just decided not to go. I asked several questions about why that day—was he sick; have other plans that interfered, too much schoolwork? No, he said, he just decided not to go. He said it was a big step and it "felt weird." I probed, further—how did it feel weird? He said he thought about it all day long, but he couldn't remember his specific thoughts. Mostly, he said, he thought that it was strange that you do something every week for your entire life and then you stop. He didn't feel guilty, or at least he didn't remember feeling guilty. If anything he might have been surprised at his lack of guilt. For eighteen years he went to Church, and even if you don't believe in the stuff, those nuns can be very effective.

When I asked him to explain further what he meant about the nuns, he went on to say that he had some great nuns as teachers as a child. He said that nuns emphasized how being Catholic meant being different from the rest of society—you *had* to go to Church; you didn't eat meat on Fridays.

By the time R was a sophomore in college, he "stopped believing in the stuff." I asked what precipitated that, and he said that he was reading fiction that "freed him to have a crisis of believe." He talked about reading science fiction, Robert Heinlein, and that crystallized the lack of meaning for him, or, rather, multiple meanings

I asked R if there was anything he missed about being Catholic. He said that there wasn't anything specific to Catholicism that he missed, but he did sometimes miss having the opportunity to regularly indulge in spiritual thought. He and his wife have thought about bringing up their kids with a religious education, and they do things to expose their children to the Bible. (His daughter cherishes a Bible given to her by his brother, who passed away). He will go to Church with his mother when she visits or when he visits her, but he can't say he looks forward to it or thinks afterwards that he misses it. He hasn't been impressed by any of "those on the pulpit" he's seen. Although many years ago there was a pastor, whose name he could not remember, at Rockefeller Chapel he liked. (He described Rockefeller Chapel as the last stop to agnosticism).

I asked R if he ever noticed any remnants of his Catholic upbringing in his current behavior or attitudes or everyday life. He said he was fascinated by this question but couldn't really think of an answer. There was a long pause while he appeared to mull it over. He doesn't feel it, but he's sure it's there. He seemed distracted by this question now, and so I let him think about it. He looked away, up into the air with a sort of exaggerated gesture of pondering. After several minutes I asked if it might be helpful if I gave him an example, to which he responded, "yes, sure!" excitedly.

I told R the story of my getting a parking ticket behind Blockbuster Video and how I was angry that this had happened. My husband (raised quasi Protestant) reprimanded me for my anger. He said it was bad enough that I had broken the rule, but since I did, I should own up to the consequences instead of being mad at [*city*] for punishing my breaking the law. When I told this story to a friend, she remarked that it was "both very Protestant of [*male name*] and very Catholic of you." By this she meant that there are all these rules in the Catholic Church, and no one ever follows them, allowing Catholics to think that it's not necessary to follow *any* rules.. This was a quite cynical assessment on my friend's part, and she herself is a lapsed Catholic. I explained that, although I didn't take this particular diagnosis seriously, until that very moment, I had never entertained the possibility that my Catholic upbringing might have had such an effect on me.

Then R said: "you've given me a lovely thing to chew on," and he explained that he thought his wife might find this very interesting as well. He went on a few stream of consciousness tangents about various personal influences in his life (his father's anger, a man he worked for in high school) but never did relate any of them in the way my friend had with my story. He said he would have to ask his wife her thoughts.

I asked if, aside from the books they give their children, there were any other religion in their lives. He said no, but he thought that organized religion wasn't really necessary for him. He thinks that ancient Chinese poetry fills whatever spiritual void he might have for not practicing any type of organized religion. He began this interest when he moved to San Francisco after college. His experiences with nature in California, he said, were the closest thing he had to any kind of spiritual experience. His spirituality is based in the earth and universe. He recalled hiking in the mountains just north of San Francisco and looking west over the Pacific Ocean (Pt. Reyes and Mt. Tamalpais) and thinking that these symbolized his spirituality. He doesn't believe in heaven or hell.

The Interviewer summarized my reaction to Sean. He was "half Catholic" at the most—skeptical and yet perceptive and tolerant. Like others in this subsample, he excuses his departure on the grounds that all religion is pretty much the same and that one is as good as the other. Chinese poetry is as useful source of religious sentiment as is any Church. He doesn't add what he might for the sake of honesty that Chinese poetry doesn't make any serious demands. Maybe the Catholicism he knew as a child didn't either He was however, one more immigrant, trying perhaps to cope with the culture he was raised in and the one in which he lived. He found neither version of Catholicism particularly satisfying.

7. Marco

Interviewer: What are your childhood memories with the Church?

R: My family was not very religious. They would only go to Church every Sunday and attend festivities and Catholic ceremonies.

I follow the Church's beliefs, but I don't believe in confession because you never know what the moral beliefs of a priest would be. I do my own thing; I pray on my own and think about God. I take the communion but I don't confess.

Interviewer: Since when don't you trust priests?

R: Since I was a child in Ecuador, I saw sexual abuse from priests towards my friends. It never happened to me but I know it happened to some other kids that I knew. That happened when I was about 10 years old, before I did my first communion and then confirmation. So you never know what priests are like, even so scandals happen in all religions. Not only the Catholic Church.

Interviewer: When we did the survey you said that it could happen that you would leave the Catholic Church. Why would you leave the Catholic Church?

R: Well, I wouldn't really leave the Catholic Church now, because I'm too old now. All religions are the same, they all believe in being good to one another. I have my own interpretation of what the religion is and I'm comfortable about it. Because of my age and because all my life I've been related to the Church, I don't think I would change my religion. It wouldn't be worth it, this is the Church I know and they are basically all the same in terms of religion. Differences among Churches are based on the administrative part so I wouldn't gain anything from going to another Church.

Interviewer: You mentioned you went to catechism when you were a child?

R: I went for 3 months to prepare for first communion in Ecuador, after that we did our confirmation. Then a few years later I came to the U.S., I've been living here for 40 years now.

What do you remember you liked when you were a child about the Church or your relationship with the Church?

I remember festivities and getting together with family. We were two families that moved from Guayaquil to Quito, from the coast to the Andes, so we use to get together for special occasions like that. I was the youngest of my siblings and liked to participate in festivities. People are more religious in Ecuador than here.

Interviewer: Why do you think religion is followed closely in Ecuador than in Chicago?

R: Is the train of life (life style), here we dedicate ourselves to work, in Ecuador people have more time to relax and to go to Church. Here is all about working and then we get lazy and don't go to Church.

There is also the problem of priests and how they behave, sexual abuse scandals happen in all religions

Interviewer: Do you think that situation could change in the future?

R: With the pope coming to the U.S. the situation should change. Priests would be reminded of their moral values. That is how things change when people are reminded of their role in the Church, priests have to come together and be reminded.

Interviewer: Do you think celibacy is a problem?

R: Yes that is the main problem because priests are human, only those who are gifted by God can control their emotions like that, and that is only a few of them. Most priests are like any other human and are in big danger when surrounded by kids and adolescents.

Have you met good priests?

Well not really, nor here or in Ecuador, you never know what they are thinking or what their moral values are. I had a friend who was a priest in Ecuador that would go from town to town asking for money and then took all the money and came to the U.S., now the authorities are looking for him.

Interviewer: Wow, and have you met any good nuns, some that you have a good memory of?

R: I had an aunt who was a nun; she was my father's sister. She gave my father a leather belt to punish us because we were too noisy. We were only being kids and she wanted to punish us. She was very mean to us, nuns are too strict.

Interviewer: Are most of your friends catholic now?

R: Most of them yes, although I have a friend who became a Mormon. He was very religious with the Catholic Church; he would read at mass and go to Church very often. I was very surprised because he suddenly said we were all mistaken and the Church was mistaken. I talked to him because I was very surprised that he had changed his beliefs like that, Mormons believe other things. But I don't think it was bad, I respect what he did because all religions are basically the same.

Interviewer: What do you think your friend would be loosing when he changes to other religion?

R: Well not much really, it's just a different Church; they all believe that we should be good. Pentecostals, Jews, Muslims, they all believe in and follow the same God. That's what I do try to be at peace, follow God.

The Catholic religion is the one with the most tradition, the oldest. It is based on tradition and is where other religions, Protestants, came from. They left the Catholic Church because of mistakes done by the clergy a long time ago.

Differences between religions are on based on details, like if you go to one school or practice one sport; you still have to be a good athlete or a good student. Same thing with religion, it doesn't matter what religion you are a part of you still have to follow God.

Interviewer: Before we finish, would you like to say something, maybe about your current Church. The place where you go nowadays?

R: I still go to Church, especially because of my wife, she is the one that makes me go. But we don't go so often, our Church is very far away now, about 15 miles away in [city]. My wife is very religious so we go to every important holiday.

***

Marco is nostalgic about religion in Ecuador, though he acknowledges the problem of sexual abuse there and the tedium of Catholic rituals. Catholics in his home country are relaxed and live a slower life but the Church itself is rigid and he never trusted priest since a childhood incident of sexual abuse (he was not the victim).

8. Lydia

She lives in a large condo building right on [park]. R is probably in her late forties, tall, thinish, and brunette. She's wearing jeans and a sweater. I had called her before the interview to tell her that I was having trouble with parking (she suggested I park in her building, which was a godsend and I would have never found it if she hadn't pointed it out). I thanked her for accommodating my lateness and she said it was no problem as she works from home.

R has a large apartment that looks out right onto the park. It's bright and sunny and inviting. The furniture looks like a combination of Pottery Barn, Pier 1, and some thing inherited from family (older stuffed library or high-backed chair, antique desk in the corner). R invited me in and asks if I need to use the restroom, which I find quite perceptive. I asked her, "How'd you know, did I have that look?" She said that she figured

I was driving around looking for parking and probably drinking coffee, and if that were her, she'd need to go to the restroom. I told her she was spot on and we both laughed. She led me to the bathroom, which she described as "part my boy friend's bathroom and potting area for my spring plants." Indeed, there were several plants in a long tub. We met back in her living room and I took a seat on the couch and she sat in the stuffed chair across the room. It being a large room, she was pretty far away, which lead later to problems with the recording, I think.

I began the IRB process and she gave consent to begin. I told her that we were doing a qualitative follow-up to the survey and we selected her because she was someone who was raised Catholic but not currently practicing. She explained that she did marketing research and that she does "some qualitative" herself and she thought this was interesting.

***

Interviewer: You took the survey last fall? Last October—you left the Catholic Church?

R: I can't say that I was ever deeply entrenched, not like Mother Theresa and suddenly lost faith. Born Catholic, went to Catholic school until second grade when family moved. Weren't ever beyond that point, go to Church every Sunday sorta Catholics. Mine was less of a sudden falling out or particular point in time denouncing, but just gradual erosion out of time to where I really consider myself a lapsed Catholic with no affinity to any Church.

Strongest memory? Um, having to bobby pin a Kleenex on my head to go to Church while I was in Catholic Church.

Interviewer: Why did you have to do that?

R: Girls had to wear a hat, and if you didn't have a hat, the nun would bobby pin a Kleenex to your head. My first realization that there was something a little silly about this organized religion stuff. Not particularly fond memories of Catholic School I sucked my thumb in the second grade, and the nun who saw me doing it made me stand up on top of the desk and do it in front of the entire class.

You hear these stories about nuns and rulers....Yeah I think my brother did get slapped with a ruler. Another thing, I remember about moving in the 7th grade, and when you do confirmation you have to take these CCD classes. Before confirmation, we all stood in line and someone approached us with a question and you had to get it right before you could be confirmed. But they asked everyone the SAME question, so if you were later in line, you had it made! (*She laughed—she has a raspy laugh, like that of a smoker or someone getting over a serious chest cold.*)

I clarified that they really did ask everyone the same question, and she laughed and said "yes!" She went on to explain that it was all rote—and remembers that about confession too, she was going to forget what she was supposed to say. "Bless me father for I have sinned it has been blank days since my last confession and these are my sins." She said she was always afraid that she was gonna mess up and get it wrong. [I thought about my niece, who made a "cheer" out of this line to help her remember, and her father was very worried that she'd walk into the confessional and say her part as a cheer, "shaking her booty."] The cat came out at this point and R stopped to say hello to the tabby, who was a bit shy.

Interviewer: When you realized that it was rote, did you have doubts about Catholicism or did these come in retrospect?

R: Pretty early on sensed it was just a routine, it was just something you did—it wasn't like.. I don't know that I every really believed or questioned whatever the answers were to those questions they asked you in CCD. I remember my mother saying (we were occasional Church goers, and by that point my parents were separated and my mom was working three jobs and had a lot of other things going on) It was just sort of a credential that my mom wanted us to get. Just stick with this until you get your confirmation—didn't put it quite like this, gotta get it checked off the list, and if you don't want to go to Church after that, fine. Just get the credential, sorta like getting your high school diploma or whatever. Communion, confirmation. Done. If you ever want to get married in the Catholic Church you gotta have that—like having a high school diploma or GED or whatever. If you're gonna be a Catholic you have to have that on your imaginary Catholic resume.

Interviewer: So, she was looking down the line? Yeah, What about other family members? Was it just your mother who wasn't into it?

R: I think my grandparents were probably more believers, they both came over from Italy, and grandmother was Italian mother in her house in New Jersey, the picture of Jesus Christ and the picture of John Kennedy (*R laughs a lot at this*). But they didn't go to Church every week either.

Interviewer: Did you go on Christmas?

R: Yeah, (*half-heartedly*) yeah, Christmas and Easter was pretty much all, maybe during Lent. We were never really big on giving up anything for Lent—not those kinds of Catholics. Well, now, we did go through a stretch when I was a kid when we didn't eat meat on Fridays—we had pizza. So, Fridays were good!

***

R has one sibling who "actually goes to Church more now. His wife is Jewish, and they have brought up the kids with an exposure to both religions, both bar mitzvahs. Mother mentioned that the younger one is going to Sunday mass. My brother has probably become—not devout by any stretch—but perhaps has a function of having kids...a spiritual and intellectual exercise. He engages his kids in rich discussion and debate and finds it good as their education as humans to see the differences between Catholicism and Judaism. He's really interested in that in Judaism that God is not infallible, whereas in Catholicism God and the Pope are infallible, and that just doesn't make sense to him. He thinks it's important for the boys to consider such issues.

R paused after I asked her if she had ever considered returning. She doesn't have any friends who are strong Catholics. She has another friend who found a survey on belief net and the three of them did it independently and discovered that they are all kind of closest to Quakers. She's not sure what that is about—probably a belief in right versus wrong, doing good and doing the right thing. They did discover that they can dance—they had been under the impression that they couldn't and so they were calling themselves the "dancing Quakers" for a while. The questions on the survey ask about social issues like abortion to overall beliefs about God. She couldn't remember exactly, it was about three years ago. She said they were all somewhere between Quaker, Jewish and Unitarian. They might have given her an index number and rank you on which religions you are closer to and she was more Muslim than she was Catholic. She can't remember how many questions or anything about their methodology, but she did enjoy doing it. One of the others who did the survey with her was a lapsed Catholic and the other is lapsed but not sure what she's lapsed from.

The other thing that she has observed about Catholicism versus other religions—some time ago within the first couple of years she lived in Chicago (twenty years) she did a tour of Churches in Chicago. One of the things that struck her and is part of the reason she doesn't feel a strong affinity to the Catholic Church—others were so, so poor and she wanted to donate to some sort of a fund, and she had to ask around to find a donation box. But then you go to a Catholic Church and it's all "golden and gilded and you can't walk another five steps without finding another collection plate." She doesn't remember the other denominations, but she didn't think there was a synagogue—but other Protestant religions that are sort of a blur for her. Even having gone to Rome, seeing the Vatican and having spent a lot of time in Europe and seeing all the Catholic duomos—they talk about doing God's work, but yet, well, the Cardinal lives a few blocks from there and he's "got a pretty nice pad!" (*more laughter*). It seems that her sense of the Catholic Church is that there is a lot of money that stays within the Church when that money could be doing more good for people, social programs actually helping. She sees other Churches that have homeless Churches and volunteer programs. The Catholic Church has a lot of fat priests driving Mercedes.

R doesn't think often about joining another religion. To the extent that she has given it any thought, she has thought about going to a Unitarian service. On an intellectual level, she has thought about it—if she's not a Catholic what is she—an agnostic, atheist etc., but she's not really sure. She's not a joiner. She does believe the Karl Marx "religion is the opiate of the masses" to a certain extent. (She made comment about it getting Obama in trouble). She believes in a belief system, right and wrong, and being a good citizen in humanity, but she doesn't think she needs to go to Church on Sunday to put that into practice.

Going back to the belief net survey...What inspired her to do it? A friend emailed it and she thought she'd do it. She and her friends have talked about being lapsed Catholics over wine. And so we thought it would be interesting, and it did spark some very interesting conversations—over their next get together for wine.

I asked her what they talked about and if they discussed their Catholic upbringing. She said sure. I asked if there were any ways that her Catholic upbringing comes to play in her life now—in any way. She had a hard time coming up with an answer and was slow in her response. She said she couldn't really articulate it, but it was good for her as a child to have a religion, to have the structure and the same sense that "they say" it's good for an abstract painter to learn true art fundamentals before you go off and become an abstract painter. It was a good part of her education, to learn about God, or some sense of what puts order in the universe and right and wrong type things. In that very raw, nebulous sense it has an impact on her life today, but she doesn't agree with the Church per se on a lot of things it provided a framework for thinking about spirituality and good versus evil.

Is there any way that you think you are still "Catholic." She couldn't really put her finger on it. I explained that although people might call themselves a lapsed something or other they find themselves doing or reacting to things in a way that might be characterized as originated from a religion—like the Protestant work ethic or Jewish guilt. She laughed at these examples, but she said that she couldn't really think of any way that happened. She said that she really didn't have a strong feeling of being Catholic ever, it was just something that you did. Go to Church sit down, stand up, go to communion, etc. But that's really it. Going back to Church for a funeral was sort of like getting back on a bike and not riding it well.

I asked her if there were any other ways she can think of that Catholicism shows up in her every day life. She paused for a moment or do and she said that she does think about every once in a while about this idea of a black mark on her soul, and while she doesn't think she has a black mark, maybe a smudge here and there (and she laughed about this). Can't think of anything bad she's done, but if she does something that isn't a Christian thing and she does think of that white soul with the little black smudges on it. "that's going on my permanent record" (and laughs some more).

None of R's friends are practicing Catholics—hard to think of anyone that practices any religions, except for a few that have kids.

I asked if there was anything else she wanted to add. She was thinking about what makes a Catholic or a lapsed Catholic. She thinks of Catholicism as being one that almost—the thing that allows a lot of Catholic to consider themselves Catholic is the ability to disassociate themselves from what the Church actually says. How many Catholics practice birth control or have had an abortion or have gotten a divorce or are married outside of the faith. Or, those that just don't do a lot of things. "If you strictly defined Catholics as those that obeyed the tenets of the Catholic Church, many there wouldn't be many of them," (she laughed again.) Maybe in that respect, Catholicism is, perhaps there's a broad continuum of what a Catholic is from a real doctrine believing on one end, to someone who has fallen so far away from it they just call themselves lapsed. And a lot of people somewhere in between who are lapsed Catholics, but they just don't know it.

We talked about how much has changed in the culture of the Church—people's opinions and attitudes toward social issues are much broader and there is some tension between the realities of people's every day lives and the teachings of the Church. R said that it is probably hard for people who were brought up in the Church to make that break. She went through the "if I'm not Catholic what am I and decided she really wasn't anything." But, she thinks that a lot of people do want to have a label. She said, "this is the town I grew up in, this is where I went to college, this is my religion, you know?" They want to feel a part of something or to have something defining. It takes her back to what she was saying earlier about her mother wanting them to have the credentials, saying they were Catholic and having the documentation. She has the documentation but it's not how she defines who they are.

What makes that important to other people, although it's not important to her, why is that important to other people? She thinks it gives people a stronger sense of identity and belonging and although she is not the most self-confident, she doesn't need that sense of identity and belonging to come from religion to the extent that some people do. In today's day and age she almost finds it bothersome or concerning that so many people so strongly draw upon religion to be part of their sense of identity because so many of the world's problems are based on the belief that "I'm right you're wrong, and mine is the right god and yours is the wrong one, and you're going to burn in hell and I'm going to kill you to get you there that much sooner. That to me—falling away from the Catholic Church, comes on two different levels—one is looking at the catholic Church as opposed to others and saying—well, there's a lot of gold and guild and fat priests driving Mercedes and the priests can't get married (and a lot that's too weird)."

On a broader level, R explained she looks at all religions—and maybe this is why the Quakers and the Jews seem more attractive to her, because they don't seem as judgmental as others. "But, you know, any religion, that so strongly wants to thump itself on the chest and say that it's the right religion and others aren't, makes me not want to belong to any of them. It's all rather silly—if we all just believed in doing good things, don't do bad things and let's all just get along." Is there one god, more than one, any at all, who cares?"

Thinking back to the original quantitative survey—the sex abuse scandal was an affirmation/reinforcement that there was something weird about this Church that has all these rules that no one seems to follow. And, how could any young man in his right mind turn to the priesthood knowing that he could never married unless a lot of them were gay or screwed up. Suspected that years ago.

Lydia is yet another immigrant, this time Italian, with a strong dislike for the Church and a harsh anticlericalism which is not present in the Latino former Catholics. She doesn't need any need of religion. For her the Church is a fat priest in an expensive and religion is a trick. It doesn't matter whether there is one God or many? Who cares?

She has the memory, however, of being publicly humiliated by a nun. How is someone like Lydia to be won back by the Church? There is a lot of pent-up anger in her that is an impenetrable wall.

9. Tino

Interviewer 2: I'm Joy.

R: How are you?

Interviewer 2: I'm fine, how are you?

R: Ah, working, working. (*laughter*)

Interviewer 2: Well, uh, I guess I'd first like to start off asking you, um, what one of your strong memories of Catholicism is.

R: What is my...I couldn't hear you.

Interviewer 2: One of your strong memories associated with Catholicism.

R: Oh, being a Catholic?

Interviewer 2: Right.

R: Uh, probably baptized. That's a good one.

Interviewer 2: How old were you when you were baptized?

R: Thirteen.

Interviewer 2: Fifteen?

R: Thirteen, right.

Interviewer 2: Thirteen? So...

R: (*inaudible*)

Interviewer 2: ... you became Catholic at age 13?

R: Yeah.

Interviewer 2: Uh, what...how was your, uh, religion before that?

R: Well, my parents never took me to Church, really.

Interviewer 2: Your parents weren't...were they Catholic?

R: Ha. Yeah, they were Catholic, but they didn't really go to Church. And I started going, you know, every Sunday at the age of fourteen.

Interviewer 2: Oh. Why did you start going, um, on your own?

R: (*inaudible*) something in my life.

Interviewer 2: Sorry?

R: I felt like I was missing something in my life.

Interviewer 1: Oh, okay.

Interviewer 2: What did you feel like was missing?

R: Well, pretty much guidance. I was known as a real troublemaker when I was younger.

Interviewer 2: Mmm hmm.

R: And I was going down the wrong path, working with the wrong things and just figured there had to be something better out there.

Interviewer 2: Do you feel like the Church provided what you were needing?

R: Oh, yeah, at that time they did.

Interviewer 2: At that time?

R: Yes.

Interviewer 2: Uh, how did things change?

R: Well, that revol...revolved around the scandal in the Church now and the way that they're handling it. I don't...I don't believe in that, so, uh, I've been going to a Christian Church with my wife.

Interviewer 2: Mmm hmm. What...what scandals do you mean? Which...the sex abuse scandals?

R: Yeah.

Interviewer 2: And...and how do you mean the way, uh, the Church reacts? What do you mean by that?

R: Well, nine times out of ten they don't kick a priest out of... out of the Church and they don't take the allegations serious the first time and it happens again and again. And that's not the way life should be done.

Interviewer 2: Mmm hmm.

Interviewer 1: Mmm hmm.

Interviewer 2: So is that the primary reason why you joined another Church?

R: Oh yes. Oh yes.

Interviewer 2: Are there any other reasons?

R: Well, because my wife's a Christian.

Interviewer 2: Mmm hmm.

R: Her uncle's a pastor.

Interviewer 2: What denomination of Christianity?

R: Uh...uh, they're Baptists.

Interviewer 2: Baptists. And, um, do you feel like that Church provides what you need?

R: Yes.

Interviewer 2: And what ex...what exactly is it that you need. Before you said guidance, but is that still the case?

R: Oh yeah. I mean, every day of your life you need...you need God.

Interviewer 2: Mmm hmm. You need God?

R: Yeah, you...you've got to have...you've got to make the right decisions, you know. Sometimes when you're struggling with, you know, life, you need somewhere to turn to (*inaudible*).

Interviewer 2: Mmm hmm. And you feel that, um, Christianity provides answers to you?

R: Yeah.

Interviewer 2: Okay. Um, so when did this happen that you joined another Church?

R: Uh, I don't know, about eight, nine years ago.

Interviewer 2: Oh. So who else influenced your Church or your decision...decision to leave?

R: Uh, my wife.

Interviewer 2: Was it mostly her?

R: Yeah, my wife. Talking with her, her uncle the pastor.

Interviewer 2: Mmm hmm.

R: Actually, I'm working on (*inaudible*) right now. (*laughter*)

Interviewer 2: Wow. Um, how did your family feel about you leaving the Catholic Church?

R: Well, my...my father really didn't care, 'cause he...he...he pretty much has the same views as I do about, you know, the whole Church situation now.

Interviewer 2: Uh huh. And...

R: And, you know...

Interviewer 2: And your mother?

R: My mother is dead.

Interviewer 1: Oh.

Interviewer 2: Oh.

R: Thankfully.

Interviewer 2: Mmm hmm. Do you have siblings?

R: Well, yeah, I got four sisters.

Interviewer 1: Oh, you're the only boy.

R: Yeah, well, we were twins, but my twin brother died when we were a year old.

Interviewer 2: Oh. And are your sisters Catholic?

R: Oh, yes.

Interviewer 2: How do they feel about you leaving the Church?

R: They understand. They're actually thinking about switching to the Christian Church as well.

Interviewer 2: Oh, why?

R: Because it all gets (*s/l*) drawn out and they live o the Bible Belt.

Interviewer 2: Oh, uh huh.

R: And...

Interviewer 2: All four of them?

R: What?

Interviewer 2: All four of your sisters live in Arkansas?

R: Yeah, they all…and my one sister just moved about a month and a half ago.

Interviewer 2: Um, so they were originally from Chicago and then they all moved to Arkansas?

R: Yeah. My…my mom and dad…my mom grew up in Arkansas.

Interviewer 2: Oh, okay.

R: Which was before she died to move back and…

Interviewer 2: I see.

R: You have to live a whole new life, though (*inaudible*) happy.

Interviewer 2: Okay. Is there anything that you miss about being Catholic?

R: No, not really.

Interviewer 2: Hmm. (*laughter*) Okay. So were you, um…so this is a Baptist Church that you belong to now. Did you go through a whole like born again thing with a new baptism and all that?

R: No, no. No.

Interviewer 2: No, okay.

R: Not yet.

Interviewer 2: Not yet. Okay.

R: (*laughter*)

Interviewer 2: Is that part of something that happens in that Church?

R: Oh, well, actually, they don't really, uh… yeah, they believe in baptism, but on a baby.

Interviewer 2: Oh, okay.

R: You know, they…they…it…

Interviewer 2: So it's not a born again…

R: See, (*inaudible*) to make the decision on their own.

Interviewer 2: I see.

R: So…so it's not like going to the Catholic Church, the baby has to be baptized right away and all that.

Interviewer 2: Hmm. Okay. So even though you were…even though your parents are Catholic, you got baptized at an older age. Do you know why your parents didn't baptize you as a young child?

R: Oh, they did it as a child, but I never went to Church, so the Church didn't see me as a member.

Interviewer 2: Okay.

R: When I was 14 and I started going to Church, you know, every Sunday... Sunday, Wednesday and Friday, every week. And... and I figured, you know, if I'm gonna do it, I might as well do it right and be baptized again.

Interviewer 2: I see. So you made that decision yourself?

R: Yes.

Interviewer 2: Um...

R: And then over the years, you know, the way the Church was being run, you know, the way they are about the money situations now...

Interviewer 2: What about the money situation? What do you mean?

R: Um, you were... at the... the Church I went to, you were bound to tithing so much of your earnings every week and if you didn't, they always gave you attitude, you know.

Interviewer 2: Mmm hmm. So how would they...

R: It was a story about money.

Interviewer 2: How do you...so if you didn't make a donation or your didn't put money in the basket or...or what?

R: Well, you know what tithing is, right/

Interviewer 2: Yeah. Yeah.

R: All right. Well that's... if you're...well, a member of the Church, you're obligated to give them so much of your check.

Interviewer 2: And if they knew that you didn't, what would happen?

R: Well, they'd give you attitude.

Interviewer 2: How...how do you mean?

Interviewer 1: Can you explain what you mean by that?

R: They...they would actually ask you, well, why didn't you make your donation this...this week.

Interviewer 2: Do you mean the priest would ask you?

R: Oh, the priest, the members. Normally, the elders of the Church.

Interviewer 2: Uh huh.

R: Uh, and I... you know, I have three kids now.

Interviewer 2: Mmm hmm. Have you ever had, um, a relationship with a priest in...in a Church?

R: Relationship?

Interviewer 2: Yes.

Interviewer 1: Yeah, like have you ever gotten to know any of the priests?

R: Yes. I...

Interviewer 2: And how did you feel about the priests that you knew? Were they friendly and welcoming?

R: Well, he was a really good guy and, uh…and he…and I told him about, you know, the way I was feeling about the Church. He goes, "I…I can't blame you for being upset." Yeah. He goes, "Just follow your heart and if you…you feel becoming Christian would serve you better with God, then do it."

Interviewer 2: So he wasn't…he didn't try to discourage you from leaving the Catholic Church?

R: Oh, well, he knew I had my mind made up.

Interviewer 1: Oh, I see.

Interviewer 2: Oh.

R: Oh, he just…he knew (*inaudible*). He's young. He still calls me on Sundays.

Interviewer 2: Mmm hmm. Have you ever thought about returning to the Catholic Church?

R: Well, at this point in my life, uh, I'm very happy with, uh, being a Christian.

Interviewer 2: Okay. There is nothing that you miss or think about?

R: No, not really. I mean, uh, the Church I go to now, it's run…my uncle's…my wife's uncle is a pastor, so I mean, we're…the Church is more like (*inaudible*) family, you know.

Interviewer 2: And you didn't feel the Catholic Church gave that to you?

R: No, not really.

Interviewer 2: Oh.

R: It wasn't the same at all.

Interviewer 1: Can you…can you explain some of the differences?

R: Well, it just…(*inaudible*) the whole Church. I mean, uh, with the Church that I'm at now, I mean, if I…if I give a dollar to their thing, you know…

Interviewer 2: Uh huh.

R: But they won't…why did you only give a dollar?

Interviewer 2: Mmm hmm.

R: Uh, and let's see, if I've got a financial problem with my…my family and me, everybody in the Church will get together and they'll take up a collection to help me.

Interviewer 2: Uh huh.

R: And if it…

Interviewer 2: And you don't see the Catholic Church doing that?

R: ...(*inaudible*) do that. Ha.

Interviewer 2: You don't think the Catholic Church would do the same for you?

R: No. Because, I mean, when I...when my mother got sick, I gave her a kidney. I was out of work for about six months and they...every Sunday, you didn't tithe again, you didn't tithe again. Where's...where's your contribution to your Church? (*laughter*)

Interviewer 1: Mmm hmm.

Interviewer 2: What kind of work do you do?

R: Construction.

Interviewer 1: Okay. So this is a to...particularly tough time these days with not very much construction going on.

R: Oh, my...I'm working on the pastor's house right now and I...I got three more members of the Church that need work on their house.

Interviewer 1: Oh, good.

R: So, I mean, they're... they're always looking out for you.

Interviewer 2: Mmm hmm. So would you say that, um, the elders of the Church, they were trying...how do you think they were trying to make you feel? Like guilty?

R: Yeah, like if...if I didn't donate to the Church, I didn't love God.

Interviewer 2: Uh huh.

R: Then when I...you know, I don't even believe that you really have to go to the Church to love God. I could love him from my home. But I just like to be around positive influences.

Interviewer 2: Right. Do you consider yourself a spiritual person?

R: Yeah, pretty much.

Interviewer 2: Mmm hmm. So do you love God from your home? Like ha...is God a presence in your daily life?

R: Oh, yeah. Oh, yeah. Every meal we eat these days and every night before bed, we say our prayers.

Interviewer 2: Oh.

Interviewer 1: And, um, you said that you started to go astray when you were young?

R: Yeah.

Interviewer 1: Can you talk about that a little bit?

R: I...it's just...I was, uh, started smoking pot and...

Interviewer 2: Mmm hmm.

R: ...getting into fights and wound up getting stabbed four times and I almost died.

Interviewer 1: Hmm.

R: And that was a big turning point.

Interviewer 1: Um, was this here in Chicago?

R: Yeah.

Interviewer 1: And, um, what party of the city did you live in?

R: Oh, West Side.

Interviewer 1: Okay.

Interviewer 2: At that time, was um…were your sisters or your parents, were they Church going?

R: No, no. My parents never really went to Church that much.

Interviewer 2: Uh huh. So you really did make the decision just to go back to Church all on your own?

R: Yes.

Interviewer 1: And…and was that as a result, you think, of…of getting, you know, of almost dying?

R: Yes.

Interviewer 2: Mmm hmm. Were there any other major events in your life that changed your spirituality or your connection to the Church?

R: Well, no, not really. The…pretty much everything that happens in my life, uh, it…it's all for a purpose and I realize that now, so…

Interviewer 2: Mmm hmm.

R: It's (s/l) slow stirring from God.

Interviewer 2: Do you have any children?

R: Yes, three children.

Interviewer 2: And they…they're raised Christian as well, I assume?

R: Yes. I…I bring them to Church. If they don't want to go to Church, they don't have to. I never…I'm…I don't force any religion on anybody now.

Interviewer 2: Mmm hmm.

R: If my son…if…if my son tells me, "I don't want to go to Church today, dad," no problem, stay home. I'll stay with you.

Interviewer 2: So why exactly do you go to Church?

R: Just to give thanks.

Interviewer 2: Sorry?

R: I…I go just to give thanks.

Interviewer 2: Oh, give thanks?

R: Yes. Every day of my life is a blessing.

Interviewer 2: Mmm hmm. And is that why you pray as well?

R: Oh, yeah.

Interviewer 1: So it sounds like this um…that this event where you almost died really had a big impact on your life and you…it's made you thankful. Would you belie…would you say that that's…it…it's still a…um, prevalent with you? Do you think about it every day?

R: Oh, yeah.

Interviewer 1: Okay. Good.

R: You never forget the day you almost died. (*laughter*)

Interviewer 2: Yeah. Do you have any, um, friends that are Catholic?

R: Oh, yeah, a couple. But they… they don't really go to Church either. (*laughter*)

Interviewer 1: Good.

Interviewer 2: Do you know why they don't go?

R: No, I've never really asked them.

Interviewer 2: They don't go to the Christian Church either?

R: They don't.

Interviewer 2: Okay.

Interviewer 1: So…so when you were growing up, did you have frie…um, did you go to Catholic school?

R: No.

Interviewer 1: No?

R: I didn't go to a Catholic school, but uh…I did go to Church when you…when you… when, uh, I was fourteen. I went to public school. (*laughter*)

Interviewer 2: Mmm.

Interviewer 1: Um, so you… you went to public schools and then did you have… did you make friends in the… Catholic friends when you were going to Church when you started going when you were fourteen?

R: Yes. And I still…I still pray for them.

Interviewer 1: Okay. And how do they feel about your not being, uh, in the Catholic Church anymore?

R: Well, they don't really say much because none of them go to Church anymore.

Interviewer 1: Oh, really?

R: (*laughter*) None of them. I mean, they…(*inaudible*) parts on this. (*laughter*)

Interviewer 1: (*laughter*) Um, do you think that any of them have… have transferred to other religions or they're just not going to Catholic Church?

R: Oh, yeah, they're…they're all still pretty much Catholic, but a couple of them turned Christian. But…

Interviewer 2: Mmm hmm. Can you tell us what you think makes someone Catholic vs., um, Christian?

R: Well, the...the religions are very similar. Um, I...I feel to be a good Christian, you've got to help everyone.

Interviewer 2: Uh huh.

R: You know, you're not supposed to turn your back on anybody and, uh, they believe in justice. I mean, with the Catholic Church, the Catholic Church doesn't believe in any justice but their own.

Interviewer 2: What do you mean?

R: I mean, if...if my next door neighbor molests a kid, they go to prison from it.

Interviewer 2: Mmm hmm.

R: If a priest does it, nothing happens. They never go to jail.

Interviewer 2: Mmm hmm.

Interviewer 1: So you think the special...they feel they have like special dispensation or something like that.

R: Yes.

Interviewer 1: And why? Like why did they start, you know... how does that work? How does that...you know, why do they think that?

R: The Catholic Church is bigger than the government. I mean, if you really think about it. (*laughter*) Because 90 percent of the...of the government is Catholic.

Interviewer 1: Mmm hmm.

R: They...they...they don't have...really have to follow any regular laws because, I mean, if something happens in the Church, it's governed by the Church.

Interviewer 2: Why do you think the Church is so powerful? Like how did that become so?

R: Uh, money. All about money.

Interviewer 2: Mmm hmm.

R: The person with the money has the power.

Interviewer 2: Do you think that the Catholic Church is helpful at all to its people?

R: Well, they...they do a lot of good, but you know, you...you can't do partially good and, you know, if you're gonna do something, you've got to do it with your whole heart. And if you've done a crime upon somebody, you've got to pay for it. You can't just say, oh, we save so many souls, it don't even matter about this. Don't worry about it.

Interviewer 2: Why do you think it is that...well, first, do you think that other denominations have, uh, sex abuse scandals as well?

R: Oh, yeah. Yeah. But the thing about that is, like, um, well, with the Colorado, uh, uh…a minister, Christian minister was caught with that young child.

Interviewer 2: Mmm hmm.

R: He got sentenced to fifteen years.

Interviewer 2: Hmm. But just the Catholic Church is so powerful that it… it has the power to cover up its…

R: Yes.

Interviewer 2: Oh. Hmm. Is there anything about the Catholic Church that you think other Churches should adopt? Any practices or beliefs that are missing in other states?

R: Oh, well, the only other religion I know of is Christian and they've pretty much got everything covered, so…

Interviewer 2: Okay.

Interviewer 1: Um, do you miss anything about being Catholic? Did we ask you that already?

R: Yes, you asked me that one.

Interviewer 1: Oh.

R: Uh, not really.

Interviewer 1: Okay.

Interviewer 2: He said no.

Interviewer 1: Okay.

R: I'm a happy Christian.

Interviewer 1: Mmm hmm.

Interviewer 2: And so there's no way you'd ever go back to the Catholic Church?

R: No, at this point I don't see it ever happening.

Interviewer 2: Mmm hmm. Great.

Interviewer 1: Okay.

Interviewer 2: Is there anything else that you'd like to tell us about your relationship with the Church either as it is right now or, um, throughout your lifetime?

R: Not really. I'm just glad that I found a religion that I could truly believe in.

Interviewer 2: Mmm hmm. Okay.

Interviewer 1: Are you um…you said that, um, the…the Church that you go to now is kind of like one big family?

R: Yes.

Interviewer 1: Um…did you ever get that feeling when you were going to the Catholic Church?

R: Not...not like this.

Interviewer 2: Like in the beginning when you were...when you were going?

R: Yeah, for a while there I was like that, you know, when I was younger.

Interviewer 2: Mmm hmm.

R: But, you know, as I started growing up and I got a job and as soon as...the second I started working, it was like their hands started coming out. It was like, oh, okay, this is why they were nice.

Interviewer 2: Mmm. So you think that...do you mean as soon as you started working they wanted your money?

R: Yeah, they wanted money.

Interviewer 2: Mmm hmm.

Interviewer 1: Mmm.

R: I had the job two weeks and the elders came up to me and said, "Um, are you gonna start tithing?" I'm like, "Huh?"

Interviewer 2: And...and did you start tithing?

R: Yeah. And I...I...I could keep it up, but um, things come up and, uh, well, I...I got sick, my wife got sick, my kid broke his arm. No insurance and...but they didn't care, they wanted the money.

Interviewer 2: Did you tithe primarily because they pressured you?

R: Yeah, pretty much.

Interviewer 2: Mmm hmm. Okay.

Interviewer 1: So you...um, okay.

Interviewer 2: Was your wife Catholic, too?

R: No, she was always into Christian.

Interviewer 2: How did you meet your wife?

R: Well, actually, I met her at a gas station. Her car broke down and I fixed it for her.

Interviewer 2: Oh. (*laughter*)

Interviewer 2: Cute story.

R: Been married going on thirteen years.

Interviewer 1: Yeah. Hmm. Okay. Um, And were you married in her Church or your Church or where were you married?

R: Uh, her Church.

Interviewer 1: Okay.

R: Well, our original wedding was at City Hall, but we kept...

Interviewer 2: Okay.

R: ...arguing over what Church to have it at. But then, uh, five years later, I took...on our anniversary, we had a big Church wedding.

Interviewer 1: Oh, okay.

Interviewer 2: So you did want to marry in the Catholic Church?

R: Uh, I can (*inaudible*) my mother, my sisters already got married.

Interviewer 2: Mmm hmm.

Interviewer 1: Your mom and your sister all got married in the Catholic Church?

R: Yes.

Interviewer 2: But after a few years of marriage you started to give up Catholicism completely and you were ready to get married in your wife's Church?

R: Yeah. My wife…I started going to Church with her.

Interviewer 2: How did you feel when you first started going to that new Church?

R: Well, surprisingly, they were very, very nice. I mean, they…they welcomed me with open arms.

Interviewer 2: Did your wife ever go to Catholic Church with you?

R: Yeah, a couple of times. She don't like it.

Interviewer 1: How come?

R: Well, she said they were all too snooty.

Interviewer 1: (*laughter*) Okay.

Interviewer 2: So they just…did they welcome her at all?

R: Not really. Kind of like…well, like they're doing up (*inaudible*).

Interviewer 2: Oh.

Interviewer 1: Why?

R: Like who's this strange lady and why is she here?

Interviewer 1: Mmm.

Interviewer 2: Hmm.

Interviewer 1: Even though they knew you?

R: Yeah.

Interviewer 2: Did anyone ever try to make her become Catholic or…

R: They asked her. Uh… she said, "Nope, happy being a Christian."

Interviewer 2: Hmm.

Interviewer 1: Okay. Um…all right. Let's see if there's any… (*inaudible*) So you said that they welcomed you with open arms the first time you went. How long was it between the first time you went to your wife's Church and when you…I mean, would you say that you're officially a member of your wife's Church now?

R: Yes.

Interviewer 1: Okay. And how long was it before…between the first time you went and you're completely becoming a member there?

R: Uh, it only took me about a month.

Interviewer 1: Okay.

R: After four Sundays of going to Church with her, I mean, I…I was totally in love with the Church.

Interviewer 2: Mmm hmm. Is it that particularly Church where her uncle is the pastor or do you think it is that denomination that you…

R: Uh, actually, just (*inaudible*) but then, I mean, there the Philippines and… well, other Christian Churches with them. Uh, well, pretty much every… every Christian Church I've been in has been the same exactly.

Interviewer 1: Is your wife Fillipino?

R: Huh?

Interviewer 1: Is your wife Fillipino?

R: No.

Interviewer 1: Oh, okay. You mentioned the Philli…

R: She's (inaudible).

Interviewer 1: You mentioned the Philippines so I was just curious.

R: Oh yeah. Yeah. They got, uh…the Philippines has a, uh, very large population of Christians.

Interviewer 2: Oh.

R: So on missionary trips.

Interviewer 1: Oh, I see.

Interviewer 2: Mmm hmm. Were you invol…so you're involved with missions at your Church?

R: Uh, once in a while.

Interviewer 2: Oh.

R: When…when…when I can afford it, you know.

Interviewer 2: Uh huh. Were you ever involved in…in the Catholic Church activities?

R: Mmm, not so much.

Interviewer 2: So did you ever, um, feel like charity or giving to the poor was…well, I know tithing, but did you ever like act in charity?

R: Oh, yeah.

Interviewer 2: And did you feel like that was part of your Catholic identity?

R: Not really because they never really impressed that upon anybody.

Interviewer 2: Oh.

R: They just…they didn't get that point across, you know?

Interviewer 2: Mmm hmm.

R: It was more like give to the Church, give to the Church. They were not, you know, like…some…once a month, my wife's uncle; he'll go preach over at the mission down uh… uh…(s/l) [name of place].

Interviewer 1: Uh huh.

R: So he'll preach there and we'll stop there and make a dinner for the…the homeless shelter.

Interviewer 1: Uh huh.

R: And that…that's true…now, that…that makes you feel good, you know?

Interviewer 1: Uh huh.

R: That's something that the…the Church promotes.

Interviewer 1: Hmm. Okay. So you said that you…after four Sundays you were fully in love with your wife's Church.

R: Yeah, I was hooked.

Interviewer 1: You were hooked. And can you describe a little bit, like from the first time you went, like what was your first impression? And you said they opened…they welcomed you with open arms. What did you think about the ceremony itself?

R: Oh, it…it was like, instead of, you know, like in a Catholic Church, it's like…

Interviewer 1: Uh huh.

R: …a priest is preaching at you, not to you. At you. In the…the Christian Church, they're preaching really personally. You know, it…every time…every sermon my wife's uncle gives us, I feel like he's talking directly to me.

Interviewer 1: Okay.

R: And that's…that's…that's important to have.

Interviewer 1: Yeah.

Interviewer 2: So…

R: In (inaudible) Church.

Interviewer 1: What's that?

R: You should come to this Church one Sunday and see what I'm talking about.

Interviewer 1: Where…where is it?

R: It's in [name of place]. It's on (s/l) [directions].

Interviewer 1: Okay.

Interviewer 2: Mmm.

Interviewer 1: And what's the name of it?

R: Faith Baptist.

Interviewer 1: Okay. Okay. So you said that, um, in the Catholic Church they were preaching at you and here you felt like…you feel like every…the…priest is…the…the pastor or the minister is talking directly to you.

R: Yes.

Interviewer 1: Are there any other differences that you noted along that…you know, that four week process?

R: Well, I don't know. It uh… the main thing about Church is to get a… to hear the message and to feel the message.

Interviewer 2: Uh huh.

R: And, you know, I wi…I wish I would have been a Christian long before this.

Interviewer 2: Uh huh.

R: I mean, it helps me in my everyday life, you know? Different words, you know…one week somebody broke into my car and, you know, it was like a…it was Friday. They broke in my car. Sunday I go to Church and the pastor's talking about stealing and I'm like, wow.

Interviewer 2: Uh huh.

R: Like, you know, forgive them. Somebody needed…somebody was…you know, it's…it's not the right thing to do, but sometimes people do the wrong thing for the right reason.

Interviewer 2: Uh huh.

R: And instead of being mad about it, I (*inaudible*) at them. Hmm.

Interviewer 1: Yeah.

Interviewer 2: Mmm hmm.

Interviewer 1: Um, and so what kind of messages did you get when you went to the Catholic Church?

R: Uh…just pretty much basically about the same, but the way…the way they, uh, preach in Church, like he's trying to jam it on you, you know?

Interviewer 1: Uh huh.

R: It's just more of a lecture than it is a lesson.

Interviewer 1: Okay.

Interviewer 2: Is there anything else that's different about the Baptist Church from the Catholic Church?

R: No, not really. Just (*inaudible*) of people. (*laughter*) Money isn't everything in this world.

Interviewer 2: True. Okay.

R: All right.

Interviewer 1: Uh, all right. Well, I think unless you've got…do you have anything else that you want to talk to us about in…

R: No, I'm pretty much happy with what I told you about.

Interviewer 1: Okay.

R: I'm pretty sure you guys understand where I was coming from.

Interviewer 1: Yeah. Yeah, that's…that's helpful. We just wanted to get a few more details and, um, and that's great. We'll let you get back to work.

R: Okay.

Interviewer 1: Um, can I confirm your address so we can send you a check?

R: Oh, yeah, and you've got to get my name right this time.

Interviewer 1: Okay. (*LAUGHTER*) All right. How do you spell your last name?

R: [*spells*]

Interviewer 1: Uh huh.

R: [*spells*].

Interviewer 1: Okay.

Interviewer 2: [*name*].

Interviewer 1: [*name*], yeah.

Interviewer 2: [*name*]. Okay.

R: Um, you've got an address there?

Interviewer 1: [*address*]?

R: Yes.

Interviewer 1: Okay. [*address*].

R: Yes.

Interviewer 1: Is there an apartment number?

R: Uh, no, it doesn't matter.

Interviewer 1: Okay.

R: We own the building.

Interviewer 1: Okay.

Interviewer 2: Okay.

Interviewer 1: All right. Thanks very much for talking to us, R.

R: You have a good day and God bless you.

Interviewer 1: You, too.

Interviewer 2: Okay, bye.

Interviewer 1: Take…take care.

R: Bye-bye.

Interviewer 2: Hmm.

Interviewer 1: Pretty straightforward.

Interviewer 2: Yeah.

Interviewer 1: We're starting to hear some of the same things over and over....

Interviewer 2: Yeah.

Interviewer 1: ...and over again. (*laughter*) I didn't realize that, um, he was...that was weird for me because he's got such a ca...not Catholic...Chicago accent, you know?

Interviewer 2: Oh, he did?

Interviewer 1:   Oh yeah. That's a...

Interviewer 2: I didn't even notice.

Interviewer 1: That's a very strong Chicago, uh...and I just...I don't put that together with like the whole Baptist rhetoric. I just...

Interviewer 2: (*inaudible*)

Interviewer 1: ...it's uh...it's weird.

Interviewer 2: (*laughter*)

Interviewer 1: It's very weird. Anyway, you were gonna say?

Interviewer 2: Just that so many people really are upset about the sex abuse scandals and the money.

Interviewer 1: Yeah, it's big.

Interviewer 2: And its cover-up.

Interviewer 1: I know nothing about the money stuff.

Interviewer 2: I don't either. I guess I felt really far removed from all that just because of where I'm from. It was just something far away that we'd hear about.

Interviewer 1: Right.

Interviewer 2: And maybe if I went to Chicago and it was like the parish next door it would have made more of an impact, but...

Interviewer 1: Well, so yesterday Jonathan and I talked to this woman who said that she had mercury poisoning and she was in the hospital for a month. And she almost died and she's... she was disabled thereafter.

Interviewer 2: Mmm hmm.

Interviewer 1: And, um, she was talking about how that experience led her start questioning...led her to start questioning like why are we here kind of thing.

Interviewer 2: Yeah.

Interviewer 1: And, um, and then she decided she wanted to have a more personal relationship with Jesus. It was almost...aside from the fact that, um...(*inaudible*).

(*end of recording*)

***

Unlike many of the respondents who still had a soft place in their hearts for the Catholic parish in which they were raised, Tino was still angry. More than any of the other respondents he resented the Church's constant emphasis on money and then became even more bitter after the sexual abuse crisis about the money was being spent on the victims. The claim on 15 percent of family income as an obligation of "tithing" particularly offended him. The man has three children, how dare the Church demand that much of this income. That seems to this observer to a reasonable anger. There is no obligation to contribute even 10 percent of one's income to the Church unless it is a parish of Levites (the Jewish priestly cast to whom the original rule of tithing applied). The clergy who announce proudly to other priests, "we tithe" are in fact quoting scripture out of context. It may be that the respondent is exaggerating the situation. In fact, especially in a culture where anti-clericalism is strong, priests are taking big risks by appearing to talk about nothing but money. Compulsion, whether formal or informal is not a good idea in the modern Church.

10. Annarosa

Female, 18-40, Less than College

Interviewer 1 and Interviewer 2 drove to the respondent's home located in [*neighborhood*] on the north side of Chicago. It is a bright morning. When we enter R's neighborhood, it is a residential area with a few empty lots. People have children playing in their small chain-linked yards. There are older folks outside their yards either cleaning or enjoying the morning. As we park and walk towards the resident's home, we notice two abandoned Churches at each corner of R's street. One is a Presbyterian and the other a Baptist Church. R's home has no yard space and is a tan-colored apartment-style home. Her home is down a small alley with a chain-linked fence dividing the building next door. We arrive at the door of the R's home. The smell of cleaning supplies (Pine Sol) wafts out when the respondent opens her door. The woman is a medium height, dark, Puerto Rican and dressed in sweats and a tee shirt. She wears no make up and her hair tied in a ponytail. She takes us upstairs to her home on the second floor. We walk past the kitchen and it is spotless. The house has a linoleum floor, which is the reason why the home has the scent of pine cleaning fluid. We sit down in her living room and take a seat on a black leather couch. Her television is playing very loudly and a TV sitcom is on. On her brown coffee table, there is a melon candle burning. It mixes with the cleaning scent. She sits on her ottoman and we begin the interview.

Overall, the respondent required a lot of prodding to answer questions.

***

Interviewer 1: What was your involvement with the Catholic Church up until now?

Respondent explains that as a child, being raised in a Catholic family, R didn't have a choice being involved with the Church. R describes the Church as: "To me it's boring." "It's just a loooong lecture. We still talk about God and everything, and I come from a Hispanic family. My kids' father is African American. I prefer to go to a Christian or a Baptist Church because there is more life to it."

Interviewer 1: So, have you always felt like it was boring as a kid?

R received her confirmation, communion, and was baptized...but, R describes that she comes from a Hispanic family and so the pressure to attend the Catholic Church has been pretty deep.

Interviewer 1: What parts of the Baptist Church make it exciting?
R: They sing; they give out testimonies; they give their past life; about abuse, or into drugs, it's just a lot of stories you can relate. You either been there or someone you know has been there.
Interviewer 1: The Catholic Church doesn't allow testimonies or singing as well?
R: They sing, but it's a different type of singing.
Interviewer 1: Yeah, so you have been to another Church then? So that gives you the difference?
R: Inspiration?
Interviewer 1: How did you get introduced to the Baptist Church?
R: The other nationalities and the African Americans...(She describes AA)...They have different things and different cultures than we do.
Interviewer 1: But do you go with a friend?

R says she use to go with a kid's father then again, a couple of months ago before her grandfather passed away. Before then, R states, "I jerked around." R lists the months out loud, "the month of December, January, and February" and R's grandfather passed away in March.

Interviewer 2: Did the Church help you through this time?

R: Its different, yeah, it keeps you up. It keeps you listening with the Church. But with the Catholic Church you listen, but you aren't really listening. It drags…it takes forever.

Interviewer 2: Do you ever go to the Catholic Services?

R: I went to one because there was a death in the family.

Interviewer 1: When your grandfather passed away, is kind of a breaking situation from the Catholic Church and the kid's father is AA? So how did he get you to go to the Baptist Church?

R: Yes he did. It was also on the TV. The Baptist Church, it's on TV. (*laughs*) So when I went, I was on T.V. (*laughter*)

Interviewer 1: So that was also an influence.

Interviewer 2: Did you go as a family?

R: I went with my two boys and his mom, his father's mom. So there was a total of four of us, five of us.

Interviewer 2: So this is fairly recent then?

R: February, before my grandfather passed away. I wasn't going before because I wasn't interested in the Catholic service, the Mass. Because like I said, it was too boring.

Interviewer 1: In terms of the Catholic Church, are there any positive memories of the Catholic Church?

R: Only my mom got married at that Church…(*phone rings and R leaves*).

(*Respondent returns from call*).

Interviewer 1: So you were saying we you had a good memory of going to the Church with your mom, talking about your mom's marriage in the Church.

R: She got married at a specific Church. She still Catholic and the same Church I got my confirmation and baptism…and I don't know what else I did, communion! That's what I did. That is the only memories I have. Anytime we have a death in the family that's where everyone goes.

Interviewer 1: So, I mean, was it a positive memory when you went confirmation and communion?

R: It was an experience. But being Hispanic, you go through these steps in your culture. I never knew another life, you know.

Interviewer 1: So what's the most appealing about the Baptist Church besides it being entertaining, connected to your own life, to the testimonies, is it easier? If your family wasn't attending, would it be more difficult to go?

R: No, it's more alive than the Catholic Mass. It's more spiritual. Sometimes when I'm listening to the priest, I'm listening to him preach it's more understandable.

Interviewer 2: Is that why you found that more appealing during your difficult time with your grandfather?

R: I feel a closer connection. I was going before then before my grandfather passed away. It's just the type of word they express that's a different Catholic Mass.

Interviewer 1: This whole experiencing with the Baptist Church is a very recent experience, were you attending the Catholic Church regularly before then?

R: Um, no not as regularly, but maybe every two to three weeks or um, on occasions like Easter, or Ash Wednesday, um, weddings or funerals.

Interviewer 2: Did you ever go because of a sense of family obligation?

R: Yeah.

Interviewer 1: What about your kids, are you bringing them up in the Catholic Church?

R: My oldest boy is baptized at that Church, um Catholic. My little one is being baptized through Christian. And that's sometime in July.

Interviewer 1: What's appealing about the Christian Church?

R: I haven't been to that Church. But it's the same as the Baptist Church. It's more bigger and more spiritual. That's the reason why, my cousin is attending that Church. Her mother is diagnosed with cancer. You pray to God and it was just a miracle, cuz she was at her deathbed, she had cancer in her eye, she only had a certain time period to live, but she came out of it. She was sick and she was going to Church. Her family was going to Church; my family was going to Church. It was a miracle.

Interviewer 1: So that convinced you the Church was worth it?

R: I can't explain. It's like a light bulb went up. I just can't explain it. It...hits you that this Church, or this religion I um is prosper.

Interviewer 2: Does the location affect how often you attend Church? There is the Pentecostal Church and Baptist Church around the corner...but is there a Catholic Church?

R: Not that I know of, the only one we go to is on Western and Congress. That's the one I go to. Most of the ones of I know of are Baptists cuz half my friends are African Americans and are Baptists and are Christians. And they're Hispanic, but some of them prefer the jumping, not the one with the Holy Ghost, not that one.

Interviewer 2: So the Christian Church where your son is being baptized, is that nearby?

R: No that one is in Indiana. She's choosing the Church because she lives in Indiana.

Interviewer 2: I remember in the original survey, we asked you about your friends. You said that only one is Catholic?

R: Yeah only one that I know of.

Interviewer 2: So most of your friends are Baptists or Christians?

R: But my family is Catholic.

Interviewer 1: Can you talk more about your family, like when you were growing up with your parents and their involvement with the Church. I mean was that the heavy influence that made you go to the Catholic Church?

R: Growing up, I wouldn't remember going to Church every Sunday. I just remember baptism. I have a younger brother, and we are nine years apart. He is twenty-one ortwenty-two, or probably twenty-three, because I'm thirty-seven. I remember when he was six months old, as far as my mom and dad, after they got married. They only went on occasions. Most of it was Mass.

Interviewer 1: What about your grandparents, do you remember any of their involvement?

R: No. Just the last time when my grandfather passed away, that was in March.

Interviewer 2: You grew up in the Chicago area?

R: Uh huh (*nodding in agreement*), I was actually raised by my grandparents because my parents were workaholics.

Interviewer 1: So do you consider yourself a spiritual or religious person?

R: I believe in God.

Interviewer 2: Would you look to religion, what do you feel you get from it?

R: I feel like that I'm by myself. I feel that people have situations worse than I do. When I go to Church, it's a relief, to hear other people's problems.

Interviewer 2: These are other people, are some of them your friends?

R: Some, but some of them strangers. I occasionally see friends from old schools, old jobs. This Church is very popular. It's called the [*Church*]. So if I don't actually sit through Church, I watch it on TV.

Interviewer 2: Is it close by?

R: No this is out in [*city*], its in the [*suburbs*].

Interviewer 1: So you watch a lot of TV that's about Church services, religion?

R: Just one.

Interviewer 1: What channel is that?

R: Channel 332.

Interviewer 1: And they have the Baptist Church where they talk about people's testimonies, experiences too?

R: yeah

Interviewer 1: Do you think because its accessible because its on TV?

R: Yeah, it makes it easier. Even my present Church, it's on TV. I don't have to be physically present. I can't make it to transportation, I just going. Hey it's easier, I watch it from here.

Interviewer 2: Are some of the Catholic masses on TV sometimes? Do you ever watch them? Or is too boring?

R: It's boring.

Interviewer 1: You said it's like a big lecture, can you explain some of the topics?

R: I don't understand it. I never did. I just don't…my mind is just not there. I mean sometimes I know little words, little phrases, bless your neighbors, I'm just not interested. Even when I went to funeral mass, it's sad, but listening to the preachers, it just drags on.

***

Annarosa, a Puerto Rican, repeats a frequent charge of the lapsed Catholics in this study—she went to Mass when she was young because her family went to Church. It was part of being Catholic. But, even then it was dull, boring. The born-again Church, even the one on television, is alive, things are happening, people are talking about their problems. Her first child was baptized in the family's Catholic Church. The one she is expecting will be baptized in his father's African American Church. Religion helps people through their problems in life, but it doesn't matter which kind of religion.

11. Juana Marie

(*No Recording*)

The interview was completed in the survey lab over the phone. The woman was very enthusiastic about the conversation. When our discussion began, she took on a very critical tone of the Church. She shared a very contemptuous view of the Catholic Church. Both WG & KD presided over the interview.

WG opened up with "Discuss how your involvement with the Catholic Church has changed throughout your life from your childhood to now. What we want to understand is how Catholicism fits into your life." R discusses being very involved with Church growing up as a child, there she attended Church every Sunday. Church was discussed in Latin and people at that time cared more about the Church. There was no corruption as what is seen today. R also explains she married a non-Catholic. Her children have gone through the whole process of confirmation, and the kids have been given a choice now that they are older. R attends Church two times a month and feels now that there is so much taken away spiritually. R feels a large request for money and there is so much to give and stuff. The Church is swaying away with the children (?).

KD asked for a clarification on what she meant by taken away spiritually. R explained when she was younger, there was more discipline, nuns and priests had control, and they had somebody to look up to. Now nuns do not wear the habit and that one is lucky if you know what one looks like. Nuns now wear every-day attire. She felt inside an inspiration that you want to go [to Church]. Now, do whatever, but give money, and the Catholic Church does not help a person.

R discusses her husband and that he knew a different faith. They were married in a Catholic Church and acknowledged certain things that swayed her a little bit. R described how they grew up in a Polish neighborhood and all they wanted was a dime or so (thirty years ago) to sit in the Church. Her husband asked why they must pay to attend Church. He wouldn't go after that and didn't feel right.

KD asked for an explanation of what is different now versus then. R explains that priests went up to the pulpit and talked—not about money—but focused on individuality, and that day in the world in everyday lives, to help people spiritually. He had respect and didn't preach or holler—he had respect for people.

WG asked about social networks regarding friends: R responded that she worked with a woman who was Catholic. Her co-worker explained that when she was younger, there was a spelling bee and they had to put their feet against the wall, and if the nuns did not like something, they would be hit with a ruler. Her friend was a very devoted Catholic and now, none of them go to Church. They do not attend because of the scandal with the children and because they are asking for money all the time. R reflects on the issue of priest and nun marriage, she did not understand why they did not marry. People are human. So many Catholics have gone to the Lutheran or Protestant faith, and some are very close friends. This non-Catholic is someone they met after they left the Church.

KD asked about the appeal of the Lutheran Church. R explains that the environment is friendlier—they greet you when you come in, know you by name, and the Church is smaller. It is not as big as the Catholic Church. There are so many things going on and if a person doesn't have clothes, they help them with money and finding a job. She has gone to the Church and goes with friends or when neighbors invite her.

WG asked more about R's parents and their influence upon her. R responds that her mom is highly religious and was devout. She acquired muscular dystrophy and this changed her attendance. Her father was an alter boy. They are from the Chicago area and are both of Polish descent. She is from the Craigan area...R has a girlfriend who married a Jewish man.

Overall, for R, there has been a steady progression to change that has led the Church to asking them for money.

WG asked about the other son and her response about the son's marriage in the Catholic Church. Her older son is married to a Catholic. The girl's mother did not push the daughter. The son was able to marry in the Church.

The youngest son is engaged and has one child. He is thirty-seven years old and his fiancé is Lutheran. She was previously married. Their child is baptized as Lutheran. R has no influence over their son because once they reach a certain age they can't dictate to them anymore.

WG inquired about R's earlier survey comments regarding gay marriage. R explained she did not believe two people of the same sex should be married. God created us male and female.

KD asked R to discuss other aspects of the Church that she did not like. R talked about birth control. Every individual should practice but the Church should stay out of it. What goes on in someone's bedroom is their business. Church should not dictate the number of children. Church will not pay for children and so have no say on that. They will not pay for clothing, food, and shelter especially with today's economy.

But to kill a child is very wrong, they can leave it at the police station, fire station, even leave it with me. Let it live. But those issues belong in our own bedroom.

KD asked next what was preventing R from making a complete break from the Church. R responded by stating that she likes going back and forth [between the Lutheran and Catholic Churches]. R experiences a different kind of priest. R harbors a sense of distrust of the priests. Her husband's Church, in the Protestant Church in [*state*], they come and hug you. It's very warm. R continues to attend Catholic Church because she was brought up Catholic, ("deep down it is instilled in me to go,") and she still believes in the same way (even though there is a distrust of priests), she can't break away from the Church. The Lord is Lord and can't break. There are some differences now the Catholic Church allows jeans and shorts. They took away the formal aspect of the Church. In the Lutheran church, the women wear slacks but they don't dress like they just woke up. They aren't coming in sloppy. Why do they go in jeans and shorts? "It's Sunday!" "I'm old school."

WG asked R to talk about the impact of her college experience on her Catholic experience. R said there was no influence. R states she attended [*junior college named*].

KD asked about the biggest difference of her early Church experience to now particularly to two issues of the first being sloppy dressing.

R explains that when she was younger, everybody got dressed up and wore a hat, and lace doilies, and would sit nice. People would dress up to go to Church. So to look inside, R at this point confessed she found it difficult to express herself. KD suggested there was a sense of cathartic release. R agreed. R continues that she did not like to share her sins with the priest What's he doing that's different than what we're doing? Years ago priests talked as a friend. Priest would serve as counseling. For example, how can a priest tell you about marriage when he is not married? R told the story of [*priest*]—her husband and she came in for marriage counseling and [*priest*] was watching a ball game, and had his feet on desk, drinking a glass of wine. He was a the nicest, good-looking priest. She always wondered why he didn't marry. (But he eventually got married a year later.)

KD asked her to expand on the second issue of the release and spiritual fulfillment. R explains that she gets the same feeling in the Lutheran Church. It's like going to a psychologist—the priest is really listening. Thinking thoughts of the Church is a sense of relief when you leave. There is a sense of letting things out—they are spiritually there and letting loose. R attends when a neighbor or friend invites her over. She has been going for one or two years.

R has seen friends leave the Catholic Church and go to Willow Creek Church (at the intersection of Algonquin and Barrington Roads). She viewed that Church as very cult like. It's held in an auditorium and they put on plays. It doesn't feel right. They take 15 percent of their paychecks and the appeal is the auditorium, putting on plays and telling stories.

Juana Maria, a Latina, wishes there was more authority in the Catholic Church like there used to be, nuns in habits, for example, and more order and discipline. On the other hand, while she is firm that she will not leave the Church, she feels free to go to other Churches because she enjoys the relaxed friendly atmosphere. She will grant her own children freedom to make religious choices when they are old enough. Like many of our other respondents, she resents the constant emphasis on money in the Catholic Church. She does not seem to realize that there is some contradiction between the old authority she wants to return and the freedom for which she yearns. Like every good Catholic, she exercises the right to be contradictory in her complaints.

12. Penelope

Interviewer 2: We're just going to ask you some background questions.

RB: That's fine.

Interviewer 1: So, maybe you can tell us a little bit about your education.

RB: Well, I was educated in England, so it's totally different to here.

Interviewer 1: Yeah.

RB: I left school at fifteen years of age. I went to two Catholic Schools, one for junior, and one you went to for when you were four until you were eleven. And then the secondary school is eleven until you were fifteen, so.

Interviewer 1: Wow.

Interviewer: Your birthday's coming up soon. How would you identify yourself in terms of your race or ethnic background?

RB: Caucasian is it? Do they call white people Caucasian? I never heard that term when I lived in England. They never used to, ever used to bother with anything like. I had no idea I was a Caucasian until I came here.

RB: I'm an atheist now, so. That comes under don't believe anymore. Birth control, I believe strongly in that and abortion. Too much politics. Really with many of them. That one, (*inaudible*)...Do you need me to say anymore or is that enough?

Interviewer 1: Um, yeah, so could you describe a little more why you decided to leave the Church?

RB: Well, you don't have a category there and (*inaudible*) when divorce.

Interviewer 1: Mhmm.

RB: I think, well, I used to be a devout Catholic, and I went to two Catholic Schools, I sang in the Church choir for eleven years, and then I ended up my first was when we ended up separating, I think when I separated from my husband I started drifting away. And then I eventually got divorced. So, this is it, you know, I gotta go cause, you know, I understood what their position was on divorce, so, you know, it's a big split, you can't reconcile it anymore after that.

Interviewer 1: Yeah.

RB: And then when I came to the U.S. and I learned a little bit about (*inaudible*), and I began to be more aware of, to my way of thinking, their idiotic stance on birth control. And I respect their position on abortion, but I mean in some instances like rape and incest, I think you gotta have it in a civilized country.

Interviewer 1: Um, your husband, was he also Catholic?

RB: He was, but he took off long before I did. (*laughter*)

RB: I don't think he, he probably left when...this is my second husband.

Interviewer 1: Right.

RB: My first one, I converted him to Catholicism if you believe. (*laughter*)

RB: In the end we ended up divorced. No, this one, my second husband, he was raised as a Catholic, and he went to, he also went to a few non-Catholic Schools, but he did go to some Catholic Schools.

Interviewer 1: Right.

RB: I think, I don't know that he was ever really that devout. He left when he was probably around late teens I would say.

Interviewer 1: Okay.

RB: Then when he got involved with me, that was the end of it. (*laughter*)

RB: I think it's more strict in England. More strict, you either, you can't be confused which part you follow...

Interviewer 1: Right.

RB: ...which seems to me to be the way here that you have to follow it down the line.

Interviewer 1: Right. So, it's either all or nothing?

RB: Yeah, yeah, you couldn't, you know, well, I don't like this little one, I'm going to put this over here, which is the whole kit and caboodle.

Interviewer 1: Right. Um, so you decided to leave the Church after your divorce, was your family supportive of the decision?

RB: Oh, don't mention them. Um, most of my, my dad really, he was really an atheist, but he hadn't got the guts to say he was. Because he went off and married my mother in a register office, and he only went and got married in the Church because one of his aunts came after him, otherwise he wouldn't have gone. And then he sent my two sisters, my sister and myself, we got sent to Catholic Schools.

Interviewer 1: Okay.

RB: But no, my family wasn't really...

Interviewer 1: No.

RB: ...at all, so.

Interviewer 1: And your mother?

RB: Well, my mother died when I was six, and then my dad remarried. My stepmother was probably quite supportive. She wasn't a Catholic though.

Interviewer 1: Okay.

RB: My dad was supposed to be, but he really wasn't.

Interviewer 1: Right.

RB: So. I don't think, it was mostly I think the influence of the Catholic Schools. You know, going to two Catholic Schools, and getting, you know, when you get all your ideals and you grow up...

Interviewer 1: Right.

Interviewer 2: Did you go to Church with your family at all?

RB: No, only on my own. Only me and my friends, and I joined the choir when I was eleven, and I was in it for eleven years. I think mine was a gradual gift to begin with because after I separated from my husband, and I still used to go to Mass for a while after we split.

Interviewer 1: Right.

RB: But then gradually, you know, you sort of, you're not really a full member anymore because you're not really supposed to go receiving Communion.

Interviewer 1: Right.

RB: If they view you as being in the state of mortal sin, so and of course if...you had to make your Easter Duties every year.

Interviewer 1: Oh.

RB: And then it goes, you stop doing that, which means you're automatically ex-communicated if you don't do that.

RB: So, I think mine was a gradual drop off.

Interviewer 1: Right, but while you were with your husband, because you had to convert, right?

RB: Yes, oh yeah, for a number of years we were both, used to go.

Interviewer 1: So, every week you'd go to Church?

RB: Used to go, yeah. But after, after the split, probably gradually.

Interviewer 1: And then you moved to the U.S.?

RB: Yes. 1974 I came here.

Interviewer 1: And you mentioned that you became influenced by women's rights?

RB: ...birth control, and somewhat of abortion. Not totally, but a good bit on abortion. But the birth control really, sort of 100 percent I was opposite to.

Interviewer 1: Mhmm. Did you have a conversation with people in the Church about these issues?

RB: No it wasn't until I came here, I became aware of those.

Interviewer 1: Oh, okay.

RB: I think when I was a kid, and all my friends at school, if you have to describe it, to me it was, you had a blind faith. You never questioned anything. You just believed in it, and that was that. And you never questioned it. And of course they didn't want you to be questioning it, did they? So, I never questioned anything when I was over there. It wasn't until I started drifting away.

RB: I imagine that happens to a lot of people who end up getting divorced or separated. They're gonna drift away somewhat, aren't they?

Interviewer 1: So, did you, after the separation, um, did you speak with someone in the Church about that process, or?

RB: No.

Interviewer 1: No?

RB: No. By the time I had come over here and started seeing a few examples of the role of women in the Church, and realized how strongly I was opposed to their positions, I never wanted anything to do with them again after that. I don't hate them or have any bitterness towards them, but I strongly oppose much of what they do.

Interviewer 2: Can you describe some examples...

RB: Pardon?

Interviewer 2: Would you describe some of these examples that you mentioned?

RB: Yes. Well, one thing strongly I've seen so many bad examples with abortion and birth control where the Catholic Church is powerful in some countries where women are so poor, so many of them end up, they cannot afford to have anymore children, and the way the Church meddles in this...I mean in some countries they can't even have an abortion. Well, you know, when they've been raped and stuff like that, to me, you can't just, I don't see why any woman should have to lose her life because, you know, be expected to bear the fruits of what some rapist has done. And there's so many countries, poor countries in the world, some of them where it's totally forbidden. They cannot...(*inaudible*) I forget which country it was, more poor underdeveloped countries where the women, and they've got no access at all. They're not allowed legal birth control. Well, to me that's crazy. They shouldn't be having children they can't afford to feed.

Interviewer 1: Right.

RB: And so, you've got a mixture of their birth control attitude, plus the, you know, I don't know how many times where they have to have an abortion.

Interviewer 1: Yeah.

RB: Which I don't like the idea, and I wish we never did have to have it, but if someone gets raped, um, for instance, or incest, or whatever, I think they should have...oh, and like in Ireland, Ireland is terrible.

Interviewer 1: Yeah?

RB: They totally dominate Ireland, and the Church is ruling. And if they want an abortion, they gotta leave, they gotta go to another country where it's legal.

Interviewer 1: Right.

RB: Like thirteen-year-old girls, and, ugh, so that's why I feel strongly on those two issues. I respect their position, but I don't agree with it. They wouldn't want me back in the flock.

Interviewer 1: So, what would you think they would have to do to get you back in the flock?

RB: Oh, I don't think they possibly could. (*laughter*)

RB: I'd like to see them change their positions. I mean, like I say, I could never hate the Church, I'm not bitter about it, I just would like to see them change their positions. I'd like to see them ordain women because it's absolutely ridiculous that they don't. I must tell you one little quote I came across, oh, I was at a women's rights conference many years ago, and there were some nuns there, and one wore a button that said, "ordain women or stop Baptizing them." To me that says it all. You're either a full and equal member or you're not.

Interviewer 1: Right.

RB: I just wish the women would leave because then they might get their act together because they've had a chronic priest shortage for how many years?

Interviewer 1: Right.

RB: How many? And they, it's not that there's anything sacred about it, it's nothing to do with the sacredness of the religion. Years and years ago, centuries ago, they used to have married priests, and they left money to their children. Well, the Church didn't like that. They wanted the money being left to the Church, so that's why they brought celibacy in. It's got nothing to do with being, and it doesn't make sense because you've got such a shortage of priests. If you had women as well, there wouldn't be a shortage, would there? They'd have enough.

RB: ...you know, when, once you do drift away and start thinking for yourself, all those years I was a blind-faith Catholic, I never questioned anything. I never, I remember somebody asking me once years ago when I was about eighteen about birth control, and I hadn't got a clue about that. So, you know, they don't educate...

Interviewer 1: Right.

RB: Well, they didn't while I was in Catholic schools. We learned... they teach us about the Church, but they didn't teach us about any of the big issues like birth control, or anything.

Interviewer 1: Even as an option?

RB: Well, nobody talked about it, didn't know it existed.

Interviewer 1: Oh.

RB: So, that was it.

Interviewer 2: You mentioned you describe yourself as an atheist, right?

RB: Yes.

Interviewer 2: So, has there ever been another Church, another religion that has attracted you?

RB: No, well, I mean I am an atheist 100 percent. If I ever did, which I never will, but if I ever did ever go back to the Church, probably sentimental value I'd go back to the Catholic Church because I knew it for so many years.

RB: And probably just as a form of being sentimental. I don't hate them, I just don't agree with their position. And I did have some, I had, I got many happy memories of, I knew some really nice priests, and I knew some wonderful nuns that raised, you know, at school, and I always respected them. And individuals within the Church, but not the Church itself.

Interviewer 1: ...as an institution...

RB: And you know, they got a load of money. They've got so much money at the Vatican you wouldn't believe. I mean they've got, they have got a lot of people, don't know how much they've got. So they're probably greedy as well, right? Most of them.

RB: But now when I see it now, the pope wears really expensive shoes, the money, you know, they have a lot of money that they, too much pomp, and I don't like all that. They should give some of it to the poor. That's my way of thinking, you know, religion, if you choose to a good purpose, you know, to help the poor and stuff. But nobody knows just how much money they have in the Vatican, do they? All these treasures they've got, and they don't tell you. They're not about to tell you, are they? (*laughter*). You see why they never want me back.

RB: In fact, most of them weren't religious at all. Maybe one or two that were perhaps Lutheran or something, which I know absolutely nothing about. The only Church I really know a lot about is the Catholic Church.

Interviewer 1: Okay.

RB: I do, especially like the ones that I think, that Southern Baptist Church where they say, about women where they pass this resolution that they submit graciously to their husbands. I thought you know what you can do with that. (*laughter*)

RB: Oh, things like that really get me, you know, so I am aware of the extremes of some of these religions. There isn't one, I don't think there's one that is not sexist. I don't believe there's one. If there is one, I'd like somebody to show me because I don't believe there is.

Interviewer 2: Do you...

RB: I believe in equality of the sexes, so, and most Churches don't have it.

Interviewer 2: Do you think there's a pattern, um, when you mentioned that most of your friends were ex-Catholics, do you think there's a pattern in that, or a reason, or is it just you feel as it's a random coincidence?

RB: The ones in England, I just had my few friends I went to school with. And I wasn't really questioning it that much when I was in England. You see it's when you start questioning it that you start thinking for yourself, and you think oh, the penny drops, you know, you think oh, well they never told us this at school. And do you know when we used to...this one Catholic school that I went to every day we used to pray for the conversion of Russia. Would you believe that? I'm thinking what the hell is that gonna do? (*laughter*)

RB: That was one of the things they'd offer up a prayer for, was the conversion of Russia. Oh, of course they're opposed to Communism. So, you see, and, you know, the kids, you don't, they sort of take advantage of your, you know, naivete and your faith, and you just don't question it. Well, of course when you get older and you have life experiences...

Interviewer 1: Right.

RB: ...and then you do start questioning it. Once you question one position of theirs, you question a lot, and then if it turns out you disagree with most of them...(*laughter*)...I'll give you one example. There was a woman I knew I used to work for [*company*] in England, and this young woman, her husband, he took off. And he took off with another woman, and she was most upset about it. Anyways, she ends up getting divorced. Right, so that was it, she'd been a devout Catholic until then. So, she figured well, that's it, I'm out. Well, her cousin, one of her cousins goes and has a child outside of being married, but she's welcome back into the Church. And there's [*name of friend*] thinking well, I didn't do anything wrong, it was my husband who took off, went off and committed adultery, and my cousin who has a baby out of wedlock, she's back in. That was the thing for her, and she said you know, she said well, it's my life, you know, I've gotta choose my life and the Church, so that's why we quit the Church.

Interviewer 1: Yeah.

RB: And it doesn't make a lot of sense when you think about it. She gets divorced, but she's out.

Interviewer 1: Yeah.

RB: Somebody has a baby out of wedlock, but they can come back.

Interviewer 2: Were you talking in terms of the divorce or the Easter Duty or both?

RB: Well, if you're not in the state of grace, there's different degrees of sins. There's venial sins, which are not too bad. If you went out and murdered somebody, that would be a mortal sin, see. And then there's, and then you see not performing your Easter Duty, they ex-communicate you for that, so is that a mortal sin? I suppose it is.

Interviewer 1: Okay.

RB: You gotta do something really bad for it to be a mortal sin. And the more mild ones are classified as venial sins.

Interviewer 2: Divorce is considered a mortal sin?

RB: Uh...I suppose it is because as far as the Catholic Church is concerned, you are married, I'm still married to my first husband for the rest of my life according to them. And according to them, once you are on their list of names, they never take you off. So they either force impression that people who left, you're still on their register. They never (*inaudible*), it always counted amongst the (*inaudible*), so that's what I, I suppose it's a mortal sin. It's not as bad as if you remarry, if your husband doesn't die...your ex-husband doesn't die, and you remarry somebody, then that would put you right out of the Church. I suppose that would be a mortal sin.

Interviewer 2: I see.

Interviewer 1: Is there a difference in terms of, um, who divorces in terms of men or?

RB: No, makes no difference, if you're a Catholic, you see, my second husband, he's a Catholic. But if you go, it doesn't make him less...because he marries me and I'm divorced, just the fact that he goes through...see because you couldn't get married in the Catholic Church.

Interviewer 1: Oh.

RB: You gotta be married somewhere else. We didn't get, you couldn't go back to the Church.

Interview 1: So the second marriage cannot happen.

RB: Well, they wouldn't, they don't recognize marriage that's outside of the Church. (*laughter*)

RB: They don't. There's a lot of places like that where once they've got your name down, in England, not here because don't know anything about it here because I've never been to any Catholic Church, but I know in England, once you're in their records, you stay there. And I mean they don't recognize your divorce you see.

Interviewer 1: Oh.

RB: They don't, you do, but they don't. As far as they're concerned, I'm still married to the first one. I've been divorced since 1976.

Interviewer 2: At that point in your life, when you were getting married for the second time, would you have wanted a Church wedding?

RB: No, by that time I was an atheist.

Interviewer 2: So you didn't really want it?

RB: No, no, I wouldn't have wanted, or the funny part was, we had to go to Canada, this was, if you ever have a few hours to spare and you want to hear the story, we had, my husband was, I was here, and he was trying to come over. So I went to, I got in touch with my congressman, and he said, passes me over to the, um, immigration people, and in the end they, I mean I was trying to do it the right way, and in the end they said oh, you can't do that. You can't get married here, you can either go to Canada or England to get married, but you can't get married here. So, I was a legal resident alien then, and he was trying to come over, so then we had to go to Canada to get married. And we had to get a lawyer in Canada to prove that I was divorced. We had to get the papers from England to Canada, and the Canadians let us get married in Canada. And after all this... (*laughter*)

RB: And I said no, that's not the case, but we didn't care about it, but somebody did, so, he was convinced that, you know, because he knew we were both Catholic, and he knew that we were divorced, that we couldn't remarry in the Church. And but he was a nice fellow, so that's where we ended up getting married in Canada, so no, but they, that's another beef I have against them. If you want to know the category, they have this ordinary people the likes of me and others, you cannot have an annulment, you have a divorce, usually it's people with money who get annulment.

Interviewer 1: Can you describe to me what's an annulment?

RB: Pardon?

Interviewer 1: What's an annulment?

RB: Well, it's ridiculous. An annulment is supposed to be where you haven't consummated the marriage, see, and it's annulled because it's never been consummated. Well, one of the Kennedy's tried to pull that trick a few years ago, and he got about three kids. And, and his wife was none too pleased about it. And he said well, she became his ex, he tried to get an annulment. Well, the terms of the annulment are supposed to be something's happened and you didn't get together, and it was never consummated. See, but that's supposed to be based on that. But how can you have somebody with two or three kids who say they want an annulment. I don't know whether he got his annulment or not. But, uh, his wife was mad as hell about it because they've got these three kids. And but you see, usually the people that get annulments are money people. Most ordinary folks, you wouldn't get an annulment, you'd have to get a divorce, and you'd have to leave the Church. So, it's not an equal thing, you know, they're basing it on how much money you've got. I never heard of, show me any poor Catholic who's ever had an annulment, they've always had a divorce. So I don't think you've got that category.

RB: But I, I don't hold out any hope for them ever doing anything any good though because, I mean, I've got a friend in Canada, and she, with all due respect, the pope, she calls him the Medieval pope. I mean, I think he is, I think she's right on that, but they can't even get away from the male chauvinism. They just can't get away from that, so they've probably changed their attitudes a little bit, and they try to throw a few bones to the women, but they still don't treat them as equals. Would you make a note somewhere if you wouldn't mind, especially if this ever gets back to the Church, one question I've asked them for years and they'll never give you a straight answer. I know what the answer is, but they won't. There's a rule that women cannot go onto the altar. Who cleans it? And the fact that women aren't allowed on the altar, but they clean the altars, and I always ask them this, priests or whoever I meet, I'll say, do you give them a papal dispensation to clean that altar, because women are not allowed on the altar. It's too sacred for them to, but they're cleaning the damn thing.

Interviewer 2: I didn't know that, that's very interesting.

RB: The men don't clean it. You don't have the priest in there cleaning the altar, the women do. But they're not allowed in there, on it.

Interviewer 2: These are women from the congregation?

RB: Only the priests and the altar boys go on the altar.

Interviewer 2: Right.

RB: ...they're supposed to be part of the Church. That's the whole point, they don't treat them as equals. And it's always women. I've never seen a man clean the altar. And the point is, if they're not allowed on there, you see what I mean. If they're not allowed on the altar, it's one of the rules, you know, why are they on there without papal dispensation. There's many of them, and they know very well what you're getting at, you know, they know where you're coming from, but they'll never answer the question. Try it, ask a few priests and unworthy bishops...

RB: And they stop accumulating money, and they looked after the poor and everything, then I'd, and then I'd have some respect for them, but not while they just accumulate money and preach to you. Anybody can preach, but if you really cared about the poor, you'd go out and help them, don't you? You do something to help them. And all these women that die from botched abortions, mostly the poor ones. And Mexico, they gotta be (*inaudible*). Wherever they hold the world, you've got poverty, you've got no legal abortion, you've got women dying in childbirth, wherever they are in power around the place, that's my number one beef against them. If I have to hate them at all, that is something, because I do feel very strongly about that. I don't think the rest of it matters, you know, you can get dressed in your fancy vestments, and go off, and whatever you do. That doesn't count. It's people's lives that count to me. And the Church is supposed to be there helping them, especially the poor, and especially the women that they, I'd like to get one of them to answer my question one day about the papal dispensation to clean the altar. Blows their minds. Try it on a few of them.

Reflections

I discovered as I read and reread the interviews that my own identity as a priest intervened to make me angry at the incompetence of so many of the Church personnel that had blundered so clumsily with young people. Once again, Catholicism had "blown it." The young people who had done the interviews were more objective than I am.[1] They had no personal involvement in the persecution of my sixth-grade sweetheart by a troubled nun. The "rules" perspective, which so perverted some Catholic ministry in the era before the Vatican Council is in retreat and the attempts of some Church leaders to repeal the council reforms cannot possibly succeed, though when a Church tries to change and then to reverse the process, it is bound to make a bad situation worse. The last respondent, poor Penelope, despite her pride that she had been excommunicated is not excommunicated. In most parishes, she and her husband would be received back with open arms. Most of the deeply troubled nuns are gone as indeed are most nuns, a tragic loss for the Church, though that's another story. There is no excuse for harshness towards young people who are only trying to find their way. To the extent that it still influences some Catholic leaders, the reason is often carelessness or lack of time. Besides, as I tell those who complain to be about the quality of leadership, I say that if Jesus wanted a perfect Church he would have turned it over to the seraphs and not to flawed, imperfect humans. On the other hand, the dictum Ecclesia *semper reformanda* (The Church must always be reformed) is not often not high on the agenda of those in authority. I learned that truth as a very young priest when an even younger teen reprimanded me for losing my temper at an obnoxious crowd of his fellows. "You're not supposed to do that," he reminded me, none too gently.

My only disagreement with my Interviewers is that I thought at first they might have overestimated the hold that the Church still has on some of its lapsed sheep, Once a Catholic, always a Catholic, but several of the lost sheep seemed quite angry in their refusal to consider even the remotely possibility of a return.

One (this one at any rate) reads the religious memoirs with a sinking feeling that the Catholic Church has failed these children of immigrants. Did Catholic leaders learn nothing from the waves of immigration during the 19th and 20th centuries? Why did it, perhaps through inattention of carelessness drive away so many young people, indeed drive them into the waiting arms of the Evangelicals? Why were bishops and priests so often eager to believe that the Evangelicals were "stealing" Catholics, luring them away from Church, when in fact from the point of view of the young people themselves the Catholic Church was simply not interested in them?

In Chicago the largest immigrant group is Mexican, ethnics with their own form of Catholicism and some clergy who understood that tradition and adjusted easily to it. Some of our respondents were clearly Mexican and reported that to be Mexican was to be Catholic and to be Catholic was to be Mexican. Moreover, they were the first of the new immigrants to Chicago and parishes were waiting for them and often became the center of the local community. Even if most of the clergy in such parishes were American born Irish, trained in the Spanish language in centers in Mexico, they were aware of problems of acculturation and were sensitive to the problems of second generation immigrants, However many of the respondents were not Mexican but members of other groups, mostly it would seem Puerto Rican, whose relationship with the Church had traditionally been different. It would also seem that many of our respondents were part of a Diaspora—Chicago Hispanics who migrated to the suburbs, sometimes directly, and became part of parishes that had perhaps a Mass or even two every Sunday at which a Spanish speaking priest (perhaps not too articulate in a recently acquired language[2]). Young people from such backgrounds were temporary guests, welcome enough perhaps, but hardly requiring extra concern. If they wanted to learn more about Catholicism, could they not enroll in a Catholic school? With a friendly, relaxed, reassuring evangelical congregation such an ad hoc arrangement could hardly compete, especially if an evangelical cleric would propose perfectly legitimate questions for which the young person had no ready answers—"Why don't priests marry?" and "Why do Catholics worship Mary?"[3] The atmosphere of such a congregation seems free and open, the people friendly and the religion filled with faith and love and attractive biblical stories. The presumptive inerrancy of the Bible is a given which no one ever questions. For a young person from an immigrant family where family control over religion and religious practice is weakening such a religion is appealing and preserves the faith and love for which the young person is looking.

Moreover, most second generation immigrants remain Catholic as the data in the statistical study prove. The lost sheep generally are not so angry at the Church that their initial departure was inevitable. Somehow the Church did not have a safety net to scoop them up. Or some of the Church's personnel did not think they were worth scooping up. My opinion about the evangelicals has improved since I began this project. They provide a religion for many of these folks that we could not or, in fact, did not. Much of what the evangelicals make available to the lost sheep are versions of what we are supposed to specialize in—community, friendship, stories—even Guadalupe is welcome. And when she comes in, the Church becomes Catholic.

Concluding Recommendations

A sociologist who reports on a controversial subject is often asked, almost immediately, "Well what do you recommend!" When the audience is mostly clergy, the question often comes in the tone of someone looking for a fight. "OK, wise guy, you know so much, tell us what to do!"

So the "recommendations" that I will offer—such as they are—will be general, based on areas of research findings, the findings whose implementation I must leave to the local clergy, constrained as they are by the theoretical dicta of liturgists, the punctilious rubricists of the Congregation for Divine Worship (or whatever it is currently called) in Rome, the busybody spies of that congregation, the complaints of parishioners, the fault finders at the local chancery, and the bright ideas of parish staff. Nonetheless, I note three areas of findings that surprised me as I directed this study and which, in proper circumstances of freedom and support from superiors are worth exploring.

The first is the enormous resource of the Catholic imagination, that great rain forest as I have called it several times from which the Church draws is history of sacramentality. There is no reason that the Mass should boring or that the laity feel that they get nothing out of it.[4] Every Sunday liturgy should be designed to make one specific point—joy, hope, reconciliation, courage under stress, etc. There should always be festivity and celebration and an invocation of sacramentals—Holy Water, incense, candles. If a layperson walks out of a Sunday liturgy and says, "That was boring!" he'd better be prepared to say why it was. There should be a committee on feedback to preaching, not as an opportunity to push the priests around, but as an occasion to enhance communication on what for most people is the most important weekly parish effort. Moreover there's nothing that will exorcise the Catholic imagination than a liturgy that drags or is too long. Few parish Masses would suffer if they were fifteen minutes shorter. Do we really need three readings at every liturgy?

Secondly, the ingenuity of a parish ought to be challenged by the finding that the youngest cohort is the most religiously enthusiastic of all Chicago Catholics. Anyone who has encountered older teens or young adults finds them quite astonishing, as did sociologist Christian Smith who reports that this enthusiasm exists despite the low levels of investment of personnel and money in young people yet there are only five teen clubs in the Archdiocese and no more than five young adult programs. If there is to be any more research on Catholics in Chicago, it might well concentrate on those between fifteen and thirty. Patently, that won't happen. Yet the Church might at least give some sign that is aware of this enthusiasm, such as perhaps involving teens and young adults in liturgy planning. It is not likely that this most zealous cohort would be involved in planning a dull and boring liturgy.

Thirdly, the Catholic communalism reported in this volume offers the possibility that these small communities the existence of which the rectory is usually unaware could play powerful organizing centers in a community, in liturgical work or in gathering in of young people.

Finally, what is to be done in Chicago about the ethical divide among Catholics. The answer to that question must still be shrouded in darkness. The initiative must come from the leaders, but it cannot come without the insights and experiences of the married laity, as John Paul II said, "They have an indispensable contribution to the Church's self-understanding in these matters." The Curia tolerated such intervention once before and the result was the birth control encyclical, which slapped down the lay experience. However, the writings of the last two popes on human love would seem to legitimate a beginning that permits the Catholic Imagination to focus on the wonders of human sexuality.

I simply propose that those who might be the consumers of this report consider such possibilities.

Notes

1. I have no way of knowing whether any of them are Catholic. They played their cards very closely in their interviews.
2. "On Easter Greel," a Polish classmate once said to me, "I preach in three languages—Polish, English, and Spanish—all badly."
3. Many Mexican Presbyterian pastors in Chicago display Guadalupe.
4. I may suggest these recommendations in the tone of a retreat master. I don't intend to hassle or harass or rail at parish priests. In one way or another, I have been one

for fifty five years to do the Sunday liturgy, with all the other obligations which fill the days. These are recommendations which occurred to me as I wrote this report. I will try to apply them to myself in the months and years ahead.

References

Chaves, Mark, "Secularization as Declining Religious Authority," *Social Forces*, Vol. 72, No. 3, March 1994.

Hoge, Dean, William Dinges, Mary Johnson, & Juan Gonzales, Jr., *Young Adult Catholics: Religion in the Culture of Choice,* South Bend: University of Notre Dame Press, 2001.

Greeley, Andrew & Peter Rossi, *The Education of Catholic Americans,* Chicago: Aldine Publishing Co., 1966.

Greeley, Andrew, *The Hesitant Pilgrim: American Catholicism After the Council*, New York: Sheed & Ward, 1966.

Greeley, Andrew, William C. McCready, & Kathleen McCourt, *Catholic Schools in a Declining Church,* Kansas City: Sheed & Ward, 1976.

Greeley, Andrew, "Cafeteria Catholicism: Do you have to eat everything on your plate?" *U. S. Catholic*, Vol. 50, No. 1, January 1985.

Greeley, Andrew, "Why Do Catholics Stay in Church?" *The New York Times Magazine*, July 10, 1994.

Greeley, Andrew, Mike Hout, "Americans' Increasing Belief in Life after Death: Religious Competition and Acculturation?" *American Sociological Review*, Vol. 64, No. 6, December 1999.

Greeley, Andrew, *The Catholic Imagination,* Berkeley: University of California Press, 2000.

Greeley, Andrew, *The Catholic Revolution: New Wines, Old Wineskins, and the Second Vatican Council*. Berkeley: University of California Press, 2004a

Greeley, Andrew, *The Priests: A Calling in Crisis*. Chicago: University of Chicago Press, 2004b.

Greeley, Andrew & Michael Hout, *The Truth about Conservative Catholics,* Chicago: University of Chicago Press, September 2006.

Sewell, William, "Three Temporalities: Toward an 'Eventful' Sociology," *The Historic Turn in the Human Sciences*. Ann Arbor: University of Michigan, 1996.

Smith, Christian & Michael Emerson, with Patricia Snell. *Passing the Plate: Christians Don't Give Away More Money. Oxford:* Oxford University Press, 2008.

Taylor, Charles, *A Secular Age*, Harvard Press, 2007.

Warner, R. Stephen, *Gatherings in the Diaspora: Religious Communities and the New Immigration,* Philadelphia: Temple University Press, 2005.

Index